BREAKING

SOUTHERN ILLINOIS UNIVERSITY PRESS

THE CIRCLE

DEATH

AND

THE AFTERLIFE

IN BUDDHISM

Carl B. Becker

CARBONDALE AND EDWARDSVILLE

Printed in the United States of America
Edited by Tracey Moore
Designed by Chiquita Babb
Production supervised by Natalia Nadraga

09 08 07 06   7 6 5 4

Library of Congress Cataloging-in-Publication Data

Becker, Carl B., 1951–
    Breaking the circle : death and the afterlife in
Buddhism / Carl B. Becker.
        p. cm.
    Includes bibliographical references and index.
    1. Future life—Buddhism.   2. Death—Religious as-
pects—Buddhism.
    I. Title.
BQ4530.B43   1993
294.3'423—dc20   92-43710
ISBN 0-8093-1845-8   CIP
ISBN 0-8093-1932-2 (pbk.)

The paper used in this publication meets the minimum
requirements of American National Standard for Information Sciences—Permanence of Paper for Printed Library
Materials, ANSI Z39.48-1984. ∞

Contents

Contents

Preface

This is an exciting time to look at Buddhism, for Buddhism is in the process of moving from the East to the West. Whenever Buddhism moves from one culture to a different one, it finds new interpretations and new enlightenments. This book examines Buddhism's past moves from India to China, Japan, and Tibet, and contemplates the new interpretations and enlightenments that each of these moves produced, especially concerning death and the afterlife.

Recently, there have been many books looking at the problems of death and dying, like those by Elizabeth Kubler-Ross, Raymond Moody, Jr., Philippe Ariès, and Ernest Becker. There have also been many books on Buddhism, but few focusing on how Buddhists look at death and dying. This study bridges that gap. The volume of literature on non-Western death and dying has grown at a slow pace. Carol Zalesky has attempted one study of premodern visions of death; this book is the first American attempt to cover both the theory and practice of death and the afterlife from a Buddhist perspective.

Understanding Buddhist death and the afterlife is another way of understanding the Buddhist worldview: what exists and what perishes in both the visible and invisible worlds. This is the first scholarly study in English of the entire spectrum of Buddhist views of death and the afterlife ranging from India through China, Japan, and Tibet. Its emphasis is the existential impact of death and dying experiences on the Buddhist worldview.

Buddhism is full of apparent paradoxes. For example, Buddhists believe in karma and rebirth, and yet they deny the existence of permanent souls. What, then, is reborn, and why should it matter to us today? Buddhists believe that truth can be found through meditation. But how can enlightened inspiration be distinguished from illusion, and how can nonmeditating Buddhists be saved? This book treats these issues, which have confronted the leading thinkers of Buddhism down through the centuries.

The central problem in early Buddhism was how to escape the continuing cycle of birth and death. In Buddhist terms, this world of suffering and rebirth is called *samsara,* and the escape from it, *nirvana.* The question becomes: What is nirvana, and how can we reach it? Chapters 1 and 2 focus on this subject, especially as it has been discussed in Western languages.

In China and Japan, Buddhist concern with life after death moved to visions of the Pure Land and worlds to come. Was this an East Asian cultural distortion of Buddhism, or are there genuinely Buddhist bases for these interpretations? Chapters 3 and 4 examine the deathbed experiences and meditative visions of famous Chinese and Japanese Buddhists to understand their faith in salvation.

The *Book of the Dead* is central to the Tibetan Buddhist worldview. It is read into the ears of the dying and the dead to guide their journeys through the realms of consciousness intermediate between samsara and nirvana. Chapters 5 and 6 discuss the *Book of the Dead,* showing how it was shaped by the religious experiences of the Tibetans, and in turn has shaped the Buddhist understanding of the period after death.

Death and the afterlife are not merely topics of armchair speculation. They dictate how people choose to live and die. As medical facilities have improved in East Asia, issues such as euthanasia and bioethics have come to affect East Asia just as they affect the United States today. Whereas Western law and ethics tend to be grounded in Christian-based concerns about personhood and human rights, Asian law and ethics have very different presuppositions. Chapter 7 shows how Buddhist views of death and dying speak to contemporary ethical dilemmas such as suicide and euthanasia.

Portions of chapters 1 and 2 appeared in chapter 10 of *Perspectives on Death and Dying: Cross-Cultural and Multi-Disciplinary Views*, ed. by Arthur Berger et al., reprinted with permission of The Charles Press, Publishers (Philadelphia, 1989). Parts of chapters 3, 4, and 5 may be found in *The Journal for Near-Death Studies* (formerly published as *Anabiosis*) as "The Centrality of Near-Death Experiences in Chinese Pure Land Buddhism" 1 (1981), and "The Pure Land Revisited: Sino-Japanese Meditations and Near-Death Experiences of the Next World" 4 (1984). Sections of chapters 5 and 6 have also appeared in *The Journal for Near-Death Studies* as "Views from Tibet: NDEs and the *Book of the Dead*" 5.1 (1985), and in my review of Hopkins and Rinbochay's *Death, Intermediate State, and Rebirth in Tibetan Buddhism* 8.1 (1989). Parts of chapter 7 have appeared in *Philosophy East and West* as "Buddhist Views of Suicide and Euthanasia" 40.4 (1990).

Because historically women have not had the opportunity to participate in the kinds of meditative and literary practices that I describe, I have not used gender inclusive language in my discussion.

This book is the product of more than ten years' study of philosophy, science, Buddhism, Christianity, and the paranormal. The people who have helped and encouraged me in this venture are far too numerous to mention, but I should like to express my special thanks to those who have contributed most directly to making this research and writing possible. Parts of my research were conducted while on Danforth, Fulbright, and East-West Center grants, for which I am deeply grateful. Curtis

Clark, Tracey Moore, Carol Burns, and their colleagues at Southern Illinois University Press have my deep gratitude for their patient guidance and tutelage across the miles and over the years. In Japan, professors Kōshiro Tamaki and Kiyotaka Kimura of Tokyo University, Akira Kuno and Tetsuo Yamaori of the International Research Center for Japanese Studies, Yūi-chi Kajiyama and Shōtō Hase of Kyoto University, and Shinjō Kawasaki and Makio Takemura of Tsukuba University all provided valuable suggestions and insights. In Honolulu, David Chappell, Alfred Bloom, and their colleagues in the Buddhist-Christian Religions Project, as well as Reverends Yoshiaki Fujitani and Shigenori Makino and the many other Buddhist priests who work with the Buddhist Study Center, also gave invaluable encouragement and enlightenment in the course of this research. My special thanks go to P.S., who so desperately seeks to escape the wheel of rebirth, for teaching me the meaning as well as the spelling of *indispensable* and many other Japanese terms.

BREAKING THE CIRCLE

Rebirth
in Early
Buddhism

FROM ITS EARLIEST BEGINNINGS, the philosophy of Buddhism has paid considerable attention to the issues of death and the afterlife. A profound recognition of impermanence, suffering, and death is central to the philosophy of Buddhism. According to the traditional biography, Gautama Siddhartha was born and raised as a cloistered prince, protected from experiencing the ills of the world. When he finally was able to sneak out of his palace, he was deeply shocked by the sight of old, sick, and dying men. He realized that all humankind was ultimately subject to the same fate. These thoughts so troubled him that he renounced his parents, wife, child, and possessions, to seek the solution to the problem of suffering. He studied under Hindu sages, practicing austerities and meditations for many years. At last, on the verge of starvation, he resolved not to move until he had found the escape from suffering. It was during this meditation that he finally achieved enlightenment. The impermanence of life became a model for his understanding of the impermanence of all things; the suffering of disease and death became expanded into the Buddha's teaching that all material experience is ultimately suffering (Pali: *dukkha*). The enlightened Buddha concluded that the mental attitudes with which we live and die determine whether we suffer within or transcend the cycle of death and rebirth.

The Importance of Rebirth

Fundamental to Buddhist thought is the idea that life continues after death, most commonly expressed in the idea of rebirth in other human or animal bodies. If death were the ultimate end of all experiences and there were no rebirth, then suicide would be an easy solution to an existence conceived as inherently more painful than pleasurable. Moreover, if this existence were thought to be the only one that a person would experience, people might be easily encouraged to make the most hedonistic use of their few short years, rather than to overcome their desires and to transcend materialism. The Buddhist view is that this life is but one of millions of continuous lives of suffering, destined to continue indefinitely until the cycle is broken. This necessitates a path of selflessness and discipline that leads to enlightenment and freedom from the wheel of rebirth. Thus, not only death but the inescapability of survival is essential to the Buddhist philosophy.

Broadly speaking, Buddhists believe that there are two significantly different possibilities after each person's death. Either some aspect of the person's psyche will be reborn in a new body, or else the person will achieve a state called *nirvana*, which is above and beyond the realms of death and rebirth. However, there has been substantial debate about what it is that is reborn and about how the state called nirvana should be interpreted.

For cultural as well as philosophical reasons, many of the countries that have adopted Buddhism have paid much attention to its death-related ceremonies and rituals. In China and Japan, the elaborate rituals of Buddhist funerals and the practice of warriors meditating on corpses and graveyards have given Buddhism the epithet of a "religion for the dead."[1] This book is not primarily concerned with the sociocultural adaptations and formulations of Buddhism. But it is noteworthy from the outset that the issues of death and survival are more central to Buddhism than to, say, the Jewish philosophical tradition.

Culturally speaking, Buddhism has been modified by each of the countries it has entered or influenced. Its three most important divisions are the southern Theravāda or Hīnayāna school, represented by the Pali *Nikāya* scriptures, the Sino-Japanese Mahayana, including Pure Land Buddhism, and the Tibetan tantric Vajrayāna tradition. Many significant sects existed within the Theravāda, whose intricate philosophies we shall not consider here. However, in general, we might classify these three divisions as follows: the Theravādins believe that "salvation" is to be achieved through self-culture and meditative disciplines; the Mahayanists believe in salvation through the grace and power of godlike bodhisattvas; and the tantric practitioners seek salvation through esoteric practices and rituals. This first chapter is devoted to the fundamental idea of rebirth and the second chapter to understanding nirvana, as expressed in the Theravāda tradition and interpreted by modern Western scholars. In subsequent chapters, we shall see how the Chinese and Tibetan traditions developed these ideas and expanded upon them.

The Context of Early Buddhism

Even prior to the Buddha, there were numerous schools of Indian philosophy that already held dogmatic views about the nature of humanhood, the self, and the survival of death. The earliest sacred writings of the Brahmins, the *Vedas*, use the word *ātman*, which refers to the animating force, life, breath, or soul, analogous to the Greek term *psyche*. Eventually, many philosophical schools came to think of ātman as an unchanging and eternal core of personal being, the seat of consciousness that survives bodily death. This ātman is said to be reborn through numerous existences: human, subhuman, or divine. Ultimately, it was to be liberated from this cycle of rebirths by intellectually and meditatively realizing its oneness with *Brahman* (Absolute Reality), of which the ātman was essentially a tiny part.[2]

By the time of the Buddha (560–480? B.C.) many theories had arisen as to the nature, origin, and fate of the ātman (these are discussed and refuted in the *Brahmajāla Sūtra*). The major contenders in the debate seem to be the eternalists, the nihilists, and the materialists. The eternalists held that the soul was separable from the body at death like a sword from its scabbard or the pith from a blade of grass. Radhakrishnan summarizes: "If there is one doctrine more than any other which is characteristic of Hindu thought, it is the belief that there is an interior depth to the human soul which, in its essence, is uncreated and deathless and absolutely real."[3] At the same time, there were schools of nihilists who held that there was no soul at all, and of materialists who held that the soul was material and therefore necessarily dissolved at death.

These views were not merely differences in metaphysical speculation, but they resulted in drastically different ethics and lifestyles. The materialists, fearing no postmortem reward nor punishment for present deeds, tended to advocate either hedonism or passive inaction. Eternalists, on the other hand, often stressed respect for living beings and ethical self-discipline to the extent of self-mortification (*atta-kilamathanu-yoga*). Thus, the Buddha arrived on a scene already dominated by highly sophisticated philosophies concerning the soul and life after death.

The Theory of No-Soul

After a long course of austerities and meditations, the enlightened Gautama Buddha came to see that all phenomenal elements are constantly changing and impermanent (*anicca*). If everything is impermanent, then there is no unchanging essence or soul. Indeed, there is nothing in a person that can properly be identified with a soul at all; this is the theory of *anattā*, or no soul. Based on this analysis, the Buddha saw suffering (*dukkha*) to be a pervasive characteristic of material existence. He ascribed this suffering to the human longing for an unattainable permanence and to a false clinging to the mistaken notion of individual self-importance. Early Buddhists used several arguments to demonstrate this ultimate unreality of an ātman, or permanent unchanging self.

The most widely quoted of the arguments against the soul appear in the *Milindapanha*, the book of questions of Hellenistic King Menander to the erudite Buddhist monk Nāgasena on the concept of the self. Although postdating the Buddha himself, this dialogue is representative of Theravāda thought on the issue. In these illustrative but typically very repetitive conversations, Nāgasena asks the king whether a chariot can be equated to its yoke, axle, wheels, body, or flagstaffs. Of course the king denies that a chariot is equivalent to any of its components taken alone, but he defends his use of the word *chariot* as an appellation or designation of the composite entity. The conclusion to be drawn is that the word *chariot* refers to nothing other than the aggregate of material elements and that there is no innate *chariot-ness* within it.[4] (This is strikingly similar to Gilbert Ryle's illustration of a category mistake, in which a man asks to see the university after he has been shown its campus, buildings, students, and facilities. The university is nothing other than those elements working together, and the search for any other "university" is misdirected.)

Just as the chariot can be broken down into its material components with no residue of chariot-ness left over, the Buddhists teach that persons can be divided into five essential aggregates, which exhaustively describe the human being and eliminate the need for any idea of underlying soul. These five aggregates (*khandhās*) are not limited to material elements, but include sensory and psychological components, namely:

1. *rūpa*, matter or form, including earth, water, fire, and air;
2. *vedanā*, feeling, both physical and psychological;
3. *saññā*, perceptions;
4. *samkhārā*, mental states, activities, volitions;
5. *viññāna*, conscious awareness.

In a broader categorization, these aggregates can be conceptualized into those of matter/form (*rūpa*) and those of mental faculties (*nāma*). Most of the khandhās are clearly more closely related to mental processes than to matter. This is not to imply a dualistic system in which either rūpa or nāma could exist without the other. Rather, both form and faculty are interdependent on each other, and all of the khandhās are necessary in concert for there to exist what we can call a person. Since a person cannot be identified with any of the khandhās taken alone, and since the khandhās taken together exhaust the description of the person, Buddhists conclude that there is no remaining self or *atta,* outside of the interdependent complex just described.[5]

The five-khandhā analysis provides a logical, philosophical reason for rejecting selfhood. But there are even more important psychological reasons for trying to rid oneself of the conceit of selfhood—particularly the argument regarding suffering. The body (and each of the other khandhās, in turn) is first recognized to be impermanent. This impermanence is seen as a source of suffering (dukkha)—particularly suffering in terms of sickness, aging, and physical limitations. Then it is argued that it is not proper to view anything that is essentially impermanent and that causes suffering as one's own, or atta. This renunciation of the idea of selfhood is the beginning of emancipation from false cravings which lead to rebirth and thus to further suffering.[6]

With human essence, self, or soul (atta) thus analyzed out of the picture, the status of personhood after death becomes an even more serious question. Superficially, it might seem that when the body disintegrates at death, all of the other khandhās must also cease and disperse, because they are mutually interdependent. But we have already observed that the idea of rebirth is indispensable to the coherence of the Buddhist philosophy.

In fact, the Buddha taught that the action (Pali: *kamma*; Sanskrit: *karma*, meaning especially mental volition) of the dying person was in a contiguous cause-and-effect relationship with the birth of a new being. He used the term *rebirth*, as opposed to the notion of reincarnation that might imply that a single soul was reincarnated in several consecutive bodies. Rebirth, on the other hand, suggests a causal continuity between one birth and the next without requiring that the two be identified as the same person.

Buddhists hold that this teaching was not merely a crude attempt to reconcile traditional Hindu concepts of karma and reincarnation with an ethical theory that de-emphasized the centrality of the self.[7] Rather, they say that these conclusions were based on the direct paranormal knowledge of the Buddha, attained through years of meditation. Common to many meditative traditions, these extrasensory capacities enabled the Buddha to have a clear recollection of his previous lives (*pubbe-nivāsa-nussatiñana*, retrocognition) and a direct vision of the death and rebirth of beings (*cutūpapātañana*).[8]

Even the Buddha's contemporaries found his formula confusing. In order to reduce self-centeredness, the Buddha denied the reality of the self. In order to maintain the justice of the universe, he accepted the notions of karma and rebirth (that thoughts and actions have effects in future lives). But if the individual is already denied, how can there be rebirth of an individual, or a karmic reaping of the fruits of one's previous deeds?

Some interpreters try to escape this dilemma by saying that the Buddha was inconsistent or did not mean what he said. A more adequate understanding demands an answer to the question: What is it that is reborn?

Rebirth and Identity

Even in his own day, the Buddha was frequently misinterpreted by rivals as denying the doctrines of karma and rebirth. The Buddha, when questioned, explicitly denied this interpretation.[9] A different philosophical reconstruction resolves the dilemma by asserting that the karmic effects of actions influence other future generations, but not the reborn individual:

> [Buddha's] later followers endeavored to reconcile his twofold doctrine of no-permanent-soul and the moral responsibility of the individual. . . . In the Hindu view, the same individual acts and suffers in different lives; the usual *modern* Buddhist view is the same; but the strict *original* Buddhist view is altruistic, the actor being one, and the ultimate sufferer or beneficiary another individual.[10]

This is an ingenious attempt to make the idea of karma more palatable to modern behaviorists, but it flies in the face of the letter and the spirit of early Buddhist teachings. Since a permanent underlying self is denied, it is true that there is no absolute identity between the original actor and the later recipient of the fruits of that karma; just as you are not absolutely the same person now that you were when you were born.

Yet the causal connections between your childhood and your present views and experiences are unmistakable. The Buddha's theory of karma is not humanistically reducible to biological and sociological influences continuing after death. Nor is death the end of the road for the individual, or else suicide would relieve us of the suffering of existence. In Buddhism, humans die and are reborn. Their corpses and their new infancies are causally conditioned and interconnected, but not identical.

Numerous analogies in the early texts help to explain the importance of continuity over strict identity in the causal process. Nāgasena gives the case of the man who steals mangoes and later pleads that the mangoes he stole were different from the ones the owner planted. King Menander agrees that although the stolen mangoes are not identical with the ones planted, they are nevertheless causally conditioned; neither the same nor totally unrelated, they are different parts of a single causal sequence. Similarly, if a fire were to spread from a neglected campfire to an adjacent field, the burning field could be called neither the same fire nor a different fire from the campfire. Again, today's curds from yesterday's milk or the verse that the student repeats after his teacher are neither absolutely identical to nor different from the original milk or original poem. There is merely a causal sequence of events that enables us to identify one with the other or to say that one has given rise to the other. Rebirth is taken as another case of this same sort of process.[11]

Opposing the Hindu analogy of the soul as an inchworm moving from one leaf to another, relatively unchanged, the Buddhists prefer the analogy of the flame passing from wick to wick—a process lacking any permanent shape or substrate. It would appear that in answer to the question of "What is reborn?," we should accept the Buddha's answer that there is no permanent thing or stuff that flits from body to body. Yet when the five khandhās are dissolved at death, the four nonmaterial khandhās continue, like a causal current or stream of existence-energy (*bhava-sota*) to influence another material substrate—a fetus in a receptive womb.[12]

This is a far more sophisticated treatment of personal identity than that of Leibniz, which caused so much difficulty in former years by identifying fathers with sons or old generals with former footsoldiers. Clearly the sort of identity that humans have throughout their lives is a continuity of constantly changing mental and physical conditions, only identifiable with previous states through its spatiotemporal and causal contiguity.

Intermediate States

However accurate this characterization may be, it is very difficult to envision just how this immaterial causal current operates. Skeptics might argue that analogies of flames and curds are appropriate to the case of identity between a girl living in 1970 and the lady she became in 1990, where a continuous material substrate and memory are available. But it is precisely the lack of such a material substrate between the dying person and the newborn baby that renders these analogies inadequate. Even in the Buddha's day, there were strong movements to reinstate the atta, or one of the khandhās, or a subtly material self, as the stuff that moved from the corpse to the fetus. One of the most eligible candidates for the entity that is reborn is the viññāna, the khandhā most closely connected with consciousness.

Pande lists several texts that support this view, suggesting that the idea of a transmigrating viññāna is pre-Buddhist. This viññāna resembles the atta (Sanskrit: ātman) of some *Upanisads*, with the important difference that it is taken not as something permanent, but rather as an ever-changing complex.[13] Later Buddhists seized on the Buddha's use of the term *gandhabba*, the mental complex essential to the birth of a baby, as the stuff that is reborn, or they confused the psychic body (*manomayam kayam*) admitted by Buddhist meditation theory with the psychic energy that is reborn.[14]

The *vajjiputtakas* came to be known also as *Puggalavādins* because they proposed that there was a *puggala*, or self, neither identical to nor different from the khandhās and that it was this puggala that was reborn. They claimed that the Buddha's teaching of anattā did not mean that there was no self whatsoever, but simply that there was no eternal and unchanging self.[15] Buddhaghosa criticizes the Puggalavādins from the standpoint of the *Abhidharma* school, centuries later, but then he proceeds to substitute the term *bhāvānga*, or *existence factor*, in exactly the same role.[16] Asanga, in the *Yogācārabhūmi*, discusses an intermediate state between the death of the former person and the birth of the latter: "There is synonymous terminology. The term 'intermediate state' is used because it manifests in the interval between the death state and the birth state. The term *gandharva* is used . . . the term *manomaya* is used . . . the term 'resultant' [*abhinirvrtti*] is used, because it is productive in the direction of birth."[17]

Such proliferation of the very terms used to refer to the entity that is reborn and such theorizing about the intermediate states between death and rebirth are contrary to the teachings and antispeculative attitude of the Buddha. But they demonstrate that even the most outstanding classical commentators had difficulties in making sense of rebirth as an energy transfer across distances without a substrate.

Hindus like Radhakrishnan and Europeans like Grimm and Ms. Rhys-Davids suggested that the Buddha developed the anattā theory for ethical reasons but that he actually believed a sort of atta was reborn in successive bodies.[18] The cultures of China, Japan, and Tibet, lacking both the vocabulary and the sophisticated philosophical tradition of the Buddha, adopted the even more concrete idea of transmigrating souls, which we shall examine later. Historically, early Buddhism taught that there was an instantaneous rebirth of thought complexes, neither identical with nor unrelated to the dying person and not definable in terms of a single permanent underlying substance.

Let us examine the philosophical assumptions and consequences necessary to make sense of this early Buddhist doctrine of becoming and rebirth.

The Determinants of Rebirth

Since there is no single element nor substrate that is reborn, if we wish a more detailed description of rebirth, we must inquire not about the object or stuff that is reborn, but rather about the process and the factors that surround it.

The belief in rebirth into new bodies was quite widespread in India even prior to the Buddha's time, and there were already protracted debates about the implications. Some people contended that, in accordance with the law of karma, those who had done a preponderance of good deeds would be reborn in happy states and those who had done a preponderance of evil deeds would be reborn in evil states. Others, while admitting the concept of rebirth, denied the influence of karma in placing a soul in a new womb; they gave counterexamples of good men who had purportedly been reborn in evil circumstances, and evil men who were reborn in happy situations.

The Buddha discusses each of these views with Ananda in the *Mahākamma-vibhanga Sutta* (Greater Analysis of Deeds Sutra). In each of many similar sections, the Buddha asserts first of all that there are such things as good and evil deeds and that we should not allow ethical distinctions to become blurred. He supports the idea of karma even further by declaring that all deeds will ultimately produce their effects, good for good and evil for evil. He reviews the two conflicting prior views that good and evil lives inevitably produce good and evil rebirths and (conversely) that there is no correlation between actions and rebirths. The Buddha then condemns both these views as the result of overgeneralization from too limited an understanding, perhaps of psychic visualization from too limited a sample. The Buddha suggests that some deeds (kammas) are operative and others inoperative. However, the total balance sheet of good and evil deeds performed during a given lifetime is summarized by the dying person's state of mind. This is fully in accord with the Buddha's teaching that there are no underlying substances but only sequences of thought processes and that the transition from death to rebirth is but another instant in the continuity of such psychophysical processes. The Buddha explains: "At the time of dying a right view was adopted and firmly held by him; because of this, at the breaking up of the body after dying, he arises in a good bourn, a heaven world . . . or at the time of dying a false view was adopted and firmly held by him; because of this, on the breaking up of the body after dying he arises in sorrowful ways."[19]

The Buddha is not saying that these firmly held views at death are the exclusive determinants of rebirth. He is suggesting that both previous deeds and the last held thought complexes may influence rebirth, in accord with his avoidance of strict determinism and indeterminism. Historically and philosophically, this teaching was important because it opened the door to future schools of Buddhism that placed increasing emphasis on the holding of right views at the moment of death and that considered this to be more important than living a moral life in determining one's future rebirth.

A somewhat clearer explanation of the transference of energies at death is gained by placing it within the Buddhist view of conception. In the Buddhist view, sexual intercourse alone is inadequate to give rise to a conscious human being. For conception to take place, there must be present not only the male sperm and the female ovum, but also karmic energy from a third source. In Nyanatiloka's words:

> Father and mother only provide the necessary physical material for the formulation of the embryonic body. . . . The dying individual with his whole being convulsively clinging to life, at the very moment of his death, sends forth karmic energy which, like a flash of lightning, hits at a new mother's womb ready for

conception. Thus, through the impinging of karmic energies on ovum and sperm there arises, just like a precipitate, the so-called primary cell.[20]

The analogy of lightning here may be illustrative. We know that light is generally given off by physical objects glowing, burning, or reflecting other light, and we know that sounds are generally produced by collision or friction between two objects. Yet on careful analysis, a bolt of lightning is seen to be neither a physical object nor the collision of physical objects, yet it produces light and sound (thunder). In fact, by the time the light and sound reach our senses, the atmospheric processes that gave rise to the phenomenon of lightning are already stabilized, and the infinitesimal electrical particles involved are already changed into a new state in which they are no longer identifiable.

In the case of lightning, there is a visible manifestation of the imperceptibly rapid movement of invisibly small particles. In the case of rebirth, Buddhists would say that the character of the person born demonstrates the influence of life-clinging karmic forces, imperceptible except through their effects, which had existed prior to the person's birth. The Buddha sought to avoid speculative and doctrinal extremes in any direction. He said that his understanding of rebirth was gained not from metaphysical speculation nor from Hindu mythology, but from direct paranormal perception of the workings of the universe.

The Buddha maintained his teachings were completely empirical in the sense of being experience-based. He invited his students and followers to come to their own conclusions based on their own meditations. Today, most modern people seem to lack the meditational and parapsychological abilities that the Buddha gained through long years of asceticism. Yet to a certain degree, our philosophical skills may help us evaluate the Buddhist system. To begin with, concepts that are not clearly formulable or conceivable cannot merit our commitment. Moreover, we can look for the sorts of philosophical problems that might be expected to arise from the Buddha's system and the ways in which these issues might be resolved.

Difficulties with Rebirth

There are at least three obvious philosophical difficulties in the Buddhist case for rebirth: the spatiotemporal gap between the dying person and the newly conceived fetus, the population increase in the number of living beings, and the evidence for or against the rebirth theory. Let us examine the Buddhist solutions for each of these issues.

Spatiotemporal Gaps

The Buddha's descriptive analogies of rebirth are very effective in explaining how the person born is neither identical to nor different from the person who has just died. In each of them (mango, flame, wave, child becoming an adult, etc.), there is a spatiotemporal continuity from one stage to the next that enables us to identify the latter as part of the same larger process or pattern as the former. In the case of death and rebirth, however, there is no visible continuity between individual A on her deathbed and fetus B that receives the karmic life-clinging impulse upon A's death. There is at least a spatial gap between the location of the final thoughts and volitions of the dying person and the arising of the first rudimentary consciousness in the infant or fetus.

While there is no precise way of determining whether a temporal gap exists, the gap between the season of the greatest number of deaths (winter) and the season of the greatest number of births (spring) would seem to suggest a gap of months between the last thoughts of dying persons and the first thoughts of newborn babies. Moreover, there is a vast difference between the complexity of verbal and intellectual thought patterns possessed by the majority of adults at their deaths and the manifestly nonverbal and undiscriminating thought structures of all newborn infants. Thus, the continuum of death and rebirth observed paranormally by the Buddha seems to be contradicted.

A return to the Buddhist perspectives on khandhās and kamma helps us resolve these apparent dilemmas. To make sense of the Buddhist theory, we must approach it not only objectively, but from within the philosophical view of reality that the Buddhists hold. In the Buddhist view of the person, only the first of the khandhās is grossly material; the rest are fundamentally psychological characteristics, no less ontologically real for being immaterial.

Buddhists admit that all material elements return to dust at death, and therefore we are wrong to seek any *physical* traces linking a dying person with a newborn babe. The nonmaterial khandhās, however, are not limited to spatial dimensions, just as dreamscapes and ideas cannot be located spatially within a cranium.

Moreover, telepathy, clairvoyance, and out-of-body travel are accepted within the Buddhist worldview as natural results of long ascetic and meditative practice. Practice of such powers (*siddhis*) for their own sakes is condemned by the Buddha. Not only are they unconducive to enlightenment, but they are likely to distract the practitioner from more spiritual goals. While modern Westerners would consider telepathy to be an inexplicable example of causation at a distance, early Buddhists could easily accept the phenomenon of one well-trained mind reading the thoughts of another or transmitting its thoughts to one not physically present.

If we grant that thoughts themselves cannot be spatially located (although associated with a specific person) and that they can be sensed or transmitted psychically by individuals across a physical distance, then we must also concede that causation at a distance is possible in the realm of psychological phenomena. This is precisely what Buddhist rebirth theory contends: that psychological factors continue to influence one being or another uninterruptedly. More specifically, the dying person's wish for life naturally becomes associated with the baby whose psychophysical makeup is most receptive to precisely those psychic complexes. We may or may not choose to reject the theory of rebirth on other grounds, but any a priori dismissal on the basis of spatial gaps alone is eliminated by this analysis.

If we accept the early Buddhist tradition completely, the problem of temporal continuity need not arise at all. If it is held that the problem of temporal continuity does arise or that it is another aspect of the spatiotemporal causality problem, there are several possible answers to it.

First, following the analogy of the nonspatial character of consciousness outlined above, it might be argued that consciousness is essentially nontemporal. This is demonstrated by our ability to vividly remember past situations or to foresee future situations. By this line of reasoning, psychic components (khandhās) neither exist nor cease to exist when dissociated from their cranial counterparts; they simply are not amenable to temporal measurements until they are again affiliated with neurophysiological structures existing within this temporal continuum.

Another approach is that there are formless realms where old thoughts, actions, and desires (kamma) await fruition. Such a postulate is sometimes taken as a prerequisite for the acceptance of a nondeistic karma theory. It is believed that all thoughts and deeds are "stored" in some not merely physiological sense, until the situation is right for their fruition as moral reward or recompense. There need be no additional difficulty, then, in believing that the consciousness complex or karmic energy of a dying individual might be similarly "stored" temporarily until the conditions optimally suited for its rebirth occurred. However, the further mechanism of such a storage process, either for karma or for individuals, remains inexplicable to present science.

A third approach would be to suggest that consciousness is reborn immediately; not necessarily born in a human realm, but perhaps as a god, spirit, animal, or other creature whose birth passes unnoticed. In that case, there is no longer a problem of a temporal gap between the departure of consciousness from one dying body and its emergence in another body coming into existence. Buddhists recognize the existence of many invisible entities and realms not acknowledged by Western science. The fact that science does not recognize the existence of an entity no more denies its existence than did nineteenth-century ignorance of X-rays or microwaves deny the existence of those invisible entities.

If any of the above perspectives are admitted, then the period between death and rebirth can be accounted for, and the problem of spatiotemporal continuity no longer stands as an objection to the theory of rebirth.

Overpopulation

The problem of overpopulation is often raised against the doctrine of rebirth or reincarnation. The objector observes that there are more people on the earth now than a millennium ago and asks where all the souls of the new people came from. This argument rests on several assumptions that do not apply to the Buddhist theory.

In the first place, Buddhism believes neither in a temporal nor an eternal soul, as has been emphasized. Therefore, we should not imagine a condition of millions of disembodied souls waiting around in ethereal heavens for embodiment. Rather, both mind and body are evolved from material and psychological components. Over the course of millions of years, psychic complexes have evolved with ever-increasing complexity to suit their material bases. The increasingly animal tendencies of humankind, if there are such, might be taken as an indication that an ever-increasing number of animal souls are finding expression in human minds and bodies these days.

Buddhists also believe that beings dying elsewhere in the universe, on other planets or in spirit realms, may be reborn as humans. And it is possible that some dying people's thoughts influence more than one fetal organism at a time. The important point is that the Buddha recognized many realms of beings not recognized by most modern Westerners. Although these resemble those of the pre-Buddhist Upanisadic tradition, the Buddha denied that he merely copied a prior mythology. In numerous contexts and on many different occasions, he referred to his own paranormal psychic journeys to other worlds. If there indeed exist invisible beings or other worlds, then a population count of visible beings on earth alone is inadequate to invalidate the theory of rebirth.

The Buddhist view of the universe is much more comprehensive than that normally held by modern materialists. We have already observed how the Buddhist analysis of human personality into khandhās gives equal ontological footing to psychological and physiological components of a person. In its broadest categories, the Buddhist universe may be divided into three realms: things both immaterial and formless (*arūpadhātu*), those with form but only subtle matter (*rūpadhātu*), and the physical/sensual realm of form and gross matter (*kāmadhātu*).

Just as there are many classes of humans and animals within visible material realms, so there are many classes of gods, spirits, and demons in the invisible realms. It is thought that rebirth takes place in the realms of hell, ghosts, titans (*asuras*), animals, humans, and gods.[21] But it is generally held that only on the human level can people's kamma (thought and action) influence their destiny. The other levels are essentially expiatory or compensatory places where the merit or demerit of prior lives is rewarded or punished.

Neither heaven nor hell are taken to be eternal in the Christian sense. Gods and demons are also subject to causal laws and to the cycle of death and rebirth, although their lives are held to be longer than human lives. These other realms (*lokas*) are not necessarily seen as physically above or below this one, but as interpenetrating it; sometimes they are conceived as being generated by consciousness in an idealist fashion.[22]

There is some question as to whether the Buddha really believed all of the mythology behind the doctrines of heavens and hells or whether he merely taught it as a moral goad for the common people in his audience. It is clear, however, that the Buddha felt that he interacted with invisible gods and spirits and that during his meditations, he saw people born into higher or lower realms of existence depending on their karma and mental states.[23]

From our modern philosophical vantage point, we may suspect that the complex cosmology of early Buddhism was borrowed in part from the mythology of the Vedas and Upanisads.[24] However, the existence of invisible realms, whether of subtle matter or ideas, is one of many factors which defends the theory of rebirth against the objection of overpopulation. These spirit realms also stand as loci where karmas and consciousnesses have an intermediate but continuous existence until the appropriate circumstances emerge for their fruition on the gross material plane. Thus, the answer to the population problem is straightforward, if seen from the Buddhist perspective of the universe.

Verification

The difference between the intellectual structures of dying persons and those of newborn infants does seem to pose a problem in relating the two, for no newborn babe has begun to speak, write, gesture, or in any other way communicate that it has any more than the most rudimentary consciousness. Piaget, Bettelheim, and many other psychologists have attempted to trace the mental development of infants. There is widespread agreement that the newborn cannot distinguish object from object, color from color, or self from other, let alone make the kinds of logical and axiological distinctions that most mature people learn to make before they die. How can an infant's mind be anything like a dying person's?

The first and most obvious answer to this query might be that the physical (neural, cortical) apparatus of the newborn infant is simply unable to comprehend or express the full range of psychic energies that are "transmitted" from dying person to fetus. Not only have the muscles of the body not yet been trained to move, but the greater portion of the brain has not yet been taught to sort and label experience, as its first few years of education will train it to do. This need not imply that a consciousness from a former person did not contact or influence the fetal brain, but only that the former consciousness was unable to function fully through the infantile brain.

Secondly, it might be argued that the incredible trauma of coming from an essentially submarine fetal environment into a waking, walking world of objects would be enough to virtually obliterate the memories and dispositions of most individuals, as often happens in traumatic accidents. Alternatively, we might observe that Buddhists are not committed to the transmission of the entire memory set, dispositional complex, or psychic structure from the dying person to the fetus. The major thing that is transmitted is the craving for life and the emotions attendant thereto. If additional memories or talents emerge later in life, they may be attributable to the latent proclivities of the psychic complex from a previous existence, but their absence in the baby does not prove that no psychic components of the baby preexisted its recent birth.

The Buddha claimed that all of his conclusions were empirically testable or experienceable. The experiential tests required, however, depend on long-disciplined, carefully cultured psychic abilities, which many modern Westerners might doubt. Against rebirth, Westerners generally adduce the fact that very few children seem to remember their previous lives. On the other hand, even a few documentable cases might indicate the plausibility of the rebirth theory, for what is expected is not perfect memory of former lives, but simply some indications of influence.

The rebirth theory has not been shown to be logically self-contradictory. For this early Buddhist formulation to work, however, it at least demands acceptance of causality at a distance, the existence of psychic powers not dependent on physical bodies, and probably the existence of some realms other than the visible material one. If these Buddhist premises are granted, then the Buddhist theory of rebirth based on psychic continuity and influence can be rendered coherent and in that sense tenable.

The question of whether rebirth theory in fact accounts better for observed data than other theories then becomes an empirical one. There may be psychological reasons for personally adopting or rejecting the theory of karma and rebirth (e.g., the oft-cited allegation that it leads to a philosophy of resignation and stagnation), but these feelings clearly have no bearing on what is actually the nature of reality.

2

The Nirvana
Alternative

THE BUDDHA did not envision rebirth in a happy heaven as
the ultimate goal of life. Even heavenly realms, although pleasant, are causally conditioned and therefore impermanent, producing additional suffering in their demise. The common majority of suffering humanity might well wish to escape its suffering
even temporarily through a heavenly rebirth. A more enlightened perspective would suggest that the entire cycle of birth,
death, rebirth, and change is inextricably interlaced with suffering. In that case, the ultimate goal to be sought is not a temporary stay in heaven but a permanent release from the entire cycle
of birth and death.

In early Buddhism, such a release could only be obtained
from right practice and thought while in the human realm; even
the gods and demons must become human (and male) before
such freedom can be realized.[1] Therefore, although the human
realm experiences more suffering than the heavenly realms it is

privileged above all others in its access to this soteriological option: the complete escape from the wheel of rebirth.

This escape, or freedom, is generally known as nirvana (Pali: *nibbāna*). Its etymological roots suggest a definition of blowing out or extinction.[2] It is often analogized to the blowing out or extinguishing of a fire (the passions). It might seem that if all existence is suffering, then the only escape from suffering is in nonexistence. Such reasoning has led many Western interpreters to conclude that nirvana is simply the utter extinction of personality, which the Buddha sometimes explained in more palatable terms so as not to shock his listeners. Since nirvana is the final goal of Buddhist life and teaching it is essential that we come to terms with this question: Does nirvana actually imply annihilation, or rather some form of survival after death?

The early Buddhist scriptures are far from unambiguous about the meaning of nirvana. Their allusions to it tend to be more allegorical than literally descriptive. Problems of interpretation are intensified when we try to translate the words and concepts of nirvana into the English language, in our dramatically different culture and age. One approach to understanding nirvana might be to try to put ourselves into the cultural and meditative framework in which the Buddha lived and taught, and to conduct our further analyses in Pali, but this is impractical for the majority of us. It may actually be a test of Buddhism's universality to see how it translates into other language and thought systems. Therefore, while referring frequently to the early texts, we shall concentrate on the debates of Western scholars as to the meaning and interpretation of nirvana.

Within the modern interpretations of the meaning of nirvana we may take four views as representative of the major schools of thought: (1) nirvana as annihilation; (2) nirvana as eternal life; (3) nirvana as an ethical state in this world; and (4) nirvana as a transcendent, ineffable state in which time and person are superceded.

Annihilation

Among the first modern Western interpreters of Buddhism was Eugene Burnouf, who translated the *Lotus Sutra* and other Pali and Tibetan works into French in the mid-nineteenth century. Burnouf's view of nirvana is typified by his translation of a passage in the *Avadānasatakam*: "Until finally, Vipasyin, the completely perfect Buddha, after having performed the totality of obligations of a Buddha, was like a fire of which the fuel is consumed, entirely annihilated in the element of nirvāna in which nothing remains of that which constitutes existence."[3] This analogy of extinguishing a fire or lamp becomes archetypical for annihilationist interpreters. This conclusion is based primarily on etymological grounds.

Burnouf's prize pupil, Barthelemy Saint-Hilaire, is even more severe. He argues from the premises of anattā and dukkha (that all is selfless and suffering) that the only logical escape from such conditions must be utter extinction. Saint-Hilaire sees a hidden Brahmanism in the Buddhist view, and supposes that the goals of Buddhism and Brahmanism are the same: absorption in deity. But this, too, he reduces to annihilation: "Absorption in God—especially the God of Brahmanism—is the annihilation of the personality, that is to say, true nothingness for the individual soul; and I cannot see what is to be gained from imposing this new form on the Buddhist nirvāna."[4]

Traditional Christians, who prize the unique and eternal individuality of the human soul, abhor such an absorption theory. The words of Burnouf and Saint-Hilaire are seized upon and utilized by preachers and popularizers to decry the godlessness and nihilism of Buddhism, and in turn to condemn its inferiority to the Christian vision of salvation and afterlife.

Translator Max Müller was also a friend of Burnouf's. Müller not only agrees that Buddhism is atheistic and nihilistic, but he condemns this nihilism for "hurling man into the abyss, at the very moment when he thought he had arrived at the stronghold of the eternal." However, when Müller examines the historical and textual contexts of this interpretation more critically, he comes to the conclusion that the nirvana of total extinction was a superimposition of later Abhidharma philosophers upon early Buddhist teachings.

Pointing to the fact that the Buddha continued to live after having attained nirvana, Müller concludes that the original meaning of nirvana should be understood as the extinction of desires, pleasure, and pain. So the view of annihilationists, while pertinent to some of the later schools, should not be attributed to the early Buddhists.[5]

Later scholars recognized this apparent dual aspect of nirvana: *sopadhisesa* (with remnant) and *nirupadhisesa* (without remnant) nirvana. Nirvana with remnant is the nirvana attainable within this life while the body continues to live. Nirvana without remnant is the nirvana attained at death when nothing continues on toward rebirth. R. C. Childers interprets these as two stages through which the Buddha and enlightened persons pass, and not as two doctrines formulated in different periods: "The word nirvāna is used to designate two different things, the state of blissful sanctification called Arhatship, and the annihilation of existence in which Arhatship ends."[6]

James D'Alwis joins Childers in proclaiming the doctrinal unity of the early Buddhist texts, including both the Pali Nikāyas and the Abhidharma literature. D'Alwis thus attacks Müller's proposal that there was a stage of early Buddhism in which nirvana was *not* conceived as total extinction after death. D'Alwis declares that sopadhisesa nirvana (with physical remnant), that of the still-living Buddha, should not be interpreted as true nirvana. Rather, it is a state of insight and calm based upon the psychological qualifications that will enable the Buddha or Arhat to be completely extinguished upon death.[7]

Stcherbatsky develops a different attack on Müller's idea that nirvana is something other than utter extinction of the person.

Where D'Alwis tried to show that all the early texts were unified in theme, Stcherbatsky rejects the entire Pali canon as muddle-headed religiosity, and declares that only the later *sāstra* literature is philosophically important: "Accuracy, indeed, is not to be found at all in the Pali canon. Accuracy is not its aim. It is misleading to seek accuracy there. Accuracy is found in later works belonging to the sāstra class. All Buddhist literature is divided into a sūtra class and a sāstra class. The first is popular, the second is scientific."[8]

On this reasoning, Stcherbatsky then boldly contends that the sāstras are the only texts of Buddhism worthy of careful study; the truth of Buddhism is to be sought not in the hearsay discourses of Gautama but in the "scientific" commentaries of Nāgārjuna and Vasubandhu. Based on these sāstras, Stcherbatsky denies that any element or state exists in nirvana or that there is any branch of Buddhism which does not take the quiescence of total self-extinction as its final goal.[9]

The difficulties and assumptions behind these approaches of D'Alwis and Stcherbatsky are too glaring to repeat. Increasingly, the trend in modern scholarship has been to seek scrupulously the earliest words which might be genuinely attributed to the historic Gautama Siddhartha, rather than arbitrarily grouping all literature together or dividing it into structural classes. The twentieth century has made great strides towards identifying the early texts of the Biblical gospels, largely through philological and stylistic methods. Similar studies are slowly coming into their own in Buddhism as well.

While it may prove ultimately impossible to identify which words were really those of the Buddha, such studies will at least provide better bases upon which to separate early texts from late. Particularly where apparently contradictory statements are made about the same subject, such as nirvana, such textual discrimination may enable some resolution by showing which doctrines were earliest and when the conflicting theories entered.

Over the past century, the Abhidharma interpretations of
nirvana as self-annihilation took strong hold in the mind of
the Western public, especially through the works of Burnouf,
Müller, and Stcherbatsky. When oversimplified, the idea that
all existence is suffering seems to point only too clearly to the
conclusion that the escape from suffering must be nonexistence.
Moreover, interpreting Buddhism in this way created an easy
straw man for Christian missionaries to attack. Fortunately for
our understanding of Buddhism, these interpretations were not
allowed to pass unchallenged.

Eternal Life

Even within the Buddha's lifetime, his opponents were quick to
accuse him of teaching a nihilistic philosophy with a goal of
self-annihilation. The Buddha was equally insistent in countering these charges, for there had been annihilationist philosophers before him, and he scrupulously avoided their paths.
Refuting the annihilationist misinterpretations, he addressed his
monks: "[I] am accused wrongly, vainly, falsely, and inappropriately by some ascetics and Brahmins: 'A denier is the ascetic
Gautama; he teaches the destruction, annihilation, and per-
ishing of the being that now exists. . . . These ascetics wrongly,
vainly, falsely, and inappropriately accuse me of being what I
am not, O Monks, and of saying what I do not say."[10]

There are also passages which would indicate that the Buddha took a much more positive, even eternalistic view of the
nature of human existence: "I did exist in the past, not that I
did not; I will exist in the future, not that I will not; and I do
exist in the present, not that I do not."[11]

Perhaps it was their more serious encounters with passages
like these which caused Western interpreters to rethink their
original annihilationist interpretations. Some believed so
strongly in eternality that they could not accept that a religion

which denied the soul could ever have been taken seriously. Others' reinterpretations seem to be based on a more serious consideration of death and dying, accompanying their own aging and deaths.

In any case, some of the major Western interpreters of nirvana who initially understood it to mean self-annihilation revised their theories and switched to an opposite viewpoint in their later years. It is curious that such a phenomenon should be observable among not one but many of the major Buddhist scholars, most notable of whom were Müller, Oldenberg, Ms. Rhys-Davids, and LaVallée Poussin. Let us briefly review the stances and reasoning of each of these Buddhologists.

We have already alluded to Max Müller's reluctant condemnation of the nihilist tendencies of Buddhism. This conflict within Müller is easily understandable, for he regarded the Buddha as a great and inspired thinker. At the same time, he could not bring himself to believe that such a thinker would propose annihilation as the goal of existence. Müller was a pupil of Burnouf's in the mid-1840s in Paris, so his early writings reflect his master's annihilationist views. But Müller appended the condemnatory proviso that if annihilation were what the Buddha had really had in mind then his religion was not worthy of much respect. This is precisely the conclusion which many Christian teachers had reached, and the point where they were content to leave it.[12]

However, Müller continued to struggle with the problem of the meaning of nirvana, and after half a century of research he concluded that the nihilism of Burnouf was based upon the later metaphysical abstractions of the Abhidharma school of philosophers. (Of course, this was what Stcherbatsky was also to point out.) But Müller preferred the earlier dialogues of the Buddha to their later speculative interpretations. Nirvana, if extinction at all, was not extinction of existence, but only of the cravings which produce suffering. Müller ultimately interpreted nirvana as ". . . the entrance of the soul into rest; a subduing of all wishes and desires; indifference to joy and pain, good and evil; absorption of the soul in itself; and a freedom from the circle of existences from birth to death and from death to a new birth."[13] It is not completely clear just what this "absorption of the soul in itself" means to Müller, but it is at least obvious that it is not annihilation. On the contrary, it is a state of freedom, rest, and indifference, if not bliss.

High in the hall of fame of Pali translators stand the names of the Rhys-Davidses: Thomas and wife Caroline Augusta Foley. Thomas Rhys-Davids, long-time editor of the Pali Text Society, held a rather agnostic view of nirvana, to which Caroline had more or less tacitly consented until his death in 1922. After her husband's death, however, Caroline launched into a period of revisionism unparalleled in Buddhist scholarship: an almost missionary campaign to document that the real meaning of Buddhism was an eternal state of blessedness. She did not attempt to deny that the word nirvana seemed to imply a state of nonbeing. Rather, she claimed that the real goal of Buddhism was not nirvana at all, but rather *attha*, a metaphysical objective. "The *attha* (goal) which [early Buddhists] taught was *not nibbana*, a vanishing less in a vanishing *atta*. It was a persistent living on in that More which saw the quest as a man becoming more in the worlds."[14]

The glorification of "persistent living on," the "More," and "the quest as a man," whatever those terms might mean, has a decidedly un-Buddhist ring to it. Caroline Rhys-Davids said that her messianic motivation sprang from a newfound conviction that no religion could become as world famous as Buddhism if it were based on a cosmic negation of human values and achievements. We might also infer a psychological attempt to deal with the death of her husband behind this new doctrine of immortality.

Few if any serious Buddhologists came to agree with Ms. Rhys-Davids' view that the goal of Buddhism was attha rather than nirvana, but she adduced numerous texts and arguments to support her case as a skilled and dedicated translator. Her arguments were valuable in demonstrating that a number of very different conclusions could be drawn from the same texts, thus serving as a warning against too-doctrinaire interpretations. Other scholars who agreed with her logic but not her hermeneutics tried to show that the goal of nirvana itself was eternalistic or soul preserving.

Hermann Oldenberg's *Buddha: Sein Leben, seine Lehre, seine Gemeinde* was first published in 1881, undergoing five revisions (until 1921) and numerous translations. Although this book was first published when Oldenberg was still in his twenties, it led to Oldenberg's elevation to the position of a leading interpreter of Buddhism in the West. During the 40 years following the publication of his *Buddha*, Oldenberg revised his position on the reason for the Buddha's silence about nirvana. In the beginning he had held that the answer to the question of the existence of the ego after death was simply, "Nirvana is annihilation." In his later years, Oldenberg came to the conclusion that the Buddhists held "an absolute as a final highest goal." E. J. Thomas interjects: "This is a withdrawal of [Oldenberg's earlier] charge that if the Buddha had drawn the last conclusion of his own principles, he would have arrived at annihilation."[15]

Oldenberg was careful to avoid dogmatism, and he fully realized that the Buddha refused to clearly answer such questions. His change of mind was not based on a reading of new texts nor on a reinterpretation of old ones, but rather on a personal reconsideration of what the silences of the Buddha should be taken to mean. Dumoulin observes: "The chief exponents of the nihilist nirvāna interpretation [include] . . . H. Oldenberg in the early edition of Oldenberg's work *Buddha*. Later Oldenberg came to the conclusion that nirvāna signifies something absolute, not in the sense of the cause of the universe, but as an absolute final goal."[16] Surely these changes of mind are not solely attributable to a failure of nerve in the face of personal aging and death, but reflect the product of a lifelong struggle to come to clearer terms with the message of the Buddha.

Yet another Buddhologist who came to change his interpretation from a nihilistic to an eternalistic one was LaVallée Poussin. In his early years, LaVallée Poussin took annihilation to be the logical consequence of the doctrine of anattā, and he treated the nihilism of the Mādhyamika school as the logically correct interpretation of the Pali texts. Later, however, he switched to the antipodal view: "Je suis actuellement très certain que le Nirvāna est une 'chose en soi,' un Absolu eschatologique, le refuge éternel."[17] Nevertheless, LaVallée Poussin advocated that Westerners continue to think of nirvana as a kind of annihilation, because Western thought patterns do not enable us to conceive of blessedness or existence apart from mental and physical objects, neither of which are present in nirvana.[18]

In short, LaVallée Poussin came to believe that there are states of blessedness and existence beyond the power of language to depict or mind to imagine until actually experienced. To avoid building mythical "castles in the air" that would not correctly describe the reality of nirvana, the Buddha remained silent. But this silence should not be taken to imply that nirvana is not a real state. If LaVallée Poussin is correct in this interpretation, it goes a long way towards explaining both the reticence of the Buddha to verbalize his understanding of nirvana and the difficulty of Westerners to see nirvana as anything other than annihilation.

These scholars all switched from annihilationist to eternalist interpretations of nirvana. Well aware of the arguments on both sides, they knew that personal preference plays a large part in one's interpretation of Buddhism. There were other scholars, however, who were more radical in their absolutistic interpretations. Their arguments tended to rest either on the a priori rejection of a negative goal within a viable religious system, or on connecting the Buddha with previous Hindu thinkers and interpreting nirvana in a Hindu context.

As early as 1863, J. B. F. Obry had written a work on nirvana in response to Saint-Hilaire specifically to deny the negative implications of Saint-Hilaire's conclusions. Obry repudiates the Mādhyamika nihilism as a distortion of original Buddhism, and argues for an interpretation of Buddhism within the context of Sāmkhya Hindu philosophy. He sees a thinking principle (*purusa*) as an eternal element in both Buddhist and Sāmkhya systems, and feels that he can resolve the meaning of nirvana without remnant along these lines:

> The thinking principle remains intact by virtue of being simple, pure, immaterial, and indissoluble. The only difference is that in the one [nirvāna with substrate], this principle still has a support, a prop, a buttress (*lingam* according to the Sāmkhyas, *Upādhi* according to the Buddhists) while in the other, it no longer has any support or reason for its existence than itself. It has become *Svayambhū*, existing in and for itself.[19]

P. E. Foucaux warmly supported Obry by tracing numerous similarities between Buddhism and pre-Buddhist Brahmanic Hinduism documenting a Brahmanic interpretation of nirvana as a principle in a state beyond form, beyond being and nonbeing.[20] On a different tack, Schrader argued that the anattā theory applies only to the five khandhās, but fails to refer to that which is absolute. The anattā theory was "thereby to prove that our real entity must not be looked for in, but beyond the world."[21] These thinkers agree in considering nirvana to refer to a positive state of Absolute Being, based on the influences and similarities they perceive between early Hindu Brahmanism or Sāmkhya and early Buddhism.

If Western scholars have seen Hinduism as a clue to a positive interpretation of nirvana, Indian scholars have been even more emphatic about this relationship. N. P. Jacobson concludes that

Indian Buddhologists "display a tendency to want to save something of the self and to interpret the Buddha as intending to destroy the narrowly regimented personality in the interest of a more inclusive truer self. . . . U San Pe defends this view with a clarity and mastery of ancient Pali texts. . . . Radhakrishnan takes this position in his translation of the Dhammapada. So does [P. L. Narasu]."[22]

The Thai Abbot Monghol-Thepmuni of Wat Paknam holds a similar view: nirvana is extinction neither of self nor of perception, but only of the compulsive motivations that bind the person to samsara (the cycles of rebirth).[23] T. R. V. Murti lists numerous adjectives applied to nirvana to demonstrate its real existence: "A reality beyond all suffering and change, unfading, still, undecaying, taintless, peaceful, blissful. It is an island, the shelter, the refuge and the goal."[24] In the West, these views have been echoed by Kieth, Grimm, Frauwallner and Hoppe.[25]

While there are many arguments stating that the Buddha did not believe in a nirvana of annihilation, the arguments defending his belief in the eternal bliss of a soul in nirvana can be summarized into three types: (1) Buddhist borrowing from Sāmkhya and/or Brahmanism, (2) the theory that anattā applies only to the khandhās (and that a soul might exist outside of them), and (3) the positive metaphors and adjectives which describe nirvana. However, none of these arguments are very strong, and they often amount to little more than a rationalization for the conviction that a great world religion could not possibly be nihilistic. There are dangers in both the annihilationist and eternalist viewpoints, as K. N. Upadhyaya appropriately comments regarding the views of Grimm, Kieth, and Radhakrishnan: "All this clearly shows that these scholars, while countering the annihilationist view of Nibbana, are carried away by their own arguments to the opposite extreme of eternalism. It is indeed, very difficult to steer clear of these two opposite views."[26] It seems that the Buddha had tried to avoid both extremes, and one way to follow him in this is a humanistic agnosticism.

An Ethical State in This World

When questioned as to whether the saint exists after death, the Buddha remained silent. Had he spoken, this debate and perhaps this chapter would be unnecessary. Because the Buddha was silent on life after death, numerous interpretations have arisen on this question. It is clear that the Buddha intended to avoid both extremes of annihilationism and eternalism. And there is widespread agreement on one point: the reason for the Buddha's silence on this question was that he felt that such speculation or knowledge did not lead to spiritual or moral advancement.

The human in this world is analogized to a man wounded by an arrow who can waste no time in asking questions about the shape and origin of the arrow and about the man who shot it. Rather, he must exert all his energy towards removing the arrow which is the immediate cause of his suffering. Similarly, the Buddha taught a way towards relief of the suffering of this immediate material existence, not a system of metaphysics. It is at least clear that the circle of birth, death, and rebirth can be broken if desires and cravings are eliminated. It can similarly be argued that the entire teaching of anattā was more to encourage a selfless moral life than to provoke discussions on the nature of a soul.[27]

These considerations lead many Buddhist scholars to the conclusion that nirvana refers not to any ontological state nor to a view of existence or nonexistence after death, but rather to an ethical state here and now. This conclusion does seem to have the happy advantage of not reading too much into the Buddha's silence, nor does it invite invidious comparisons of Buddhism with other religions.

In the mid-nineteenth century, H. T. Colebrooke was already arguing for an ethical rather than an ontological interpretation of nirvana. A true Indologist, Colebrooke saw the Buddhist teachings within a thoroughly Indian frame of reference. Yet he refused to concede that the goal of all Indian philosophy was in the eternal and transcendant. On the contrary, he believed the common aim of Hinduism and Buddhism to be the destruction of the joys, sorrows, lusts, fears, and passions which otherwise tend to dominate this worldly existence: "A happy state of imperturbable apathy is the ultimate bliss to which the Indian aspires: in this the Jaina, as well as the Bauddha, concurs with the orthodox Vedantin. . . . It is not annihilation, but unceasing apathy, which they understand to be the extinction of their saints."[28]

In this view, nirvana refers not to the extinction of existence but to the extinction of the cravings which fetter and trouble humankind. At first glance it may seem contradictory to assert that this apathy is at the same time somehow blissful. But this is precisely the conclusion which is reached if we grant the Buddhist premises: (1) The realm of material acquisitiveness is essentially suffering, (2) The opposite of material acquisitiveness is selfless apathy, and therefore (3) The opposite of suffering is peace and in that sense, bliss. Not a flighty transcendence, but a self-disciplined detachment seems the best way to avoid the struggles and sufferings of this world. Thomas Rhys-Davids supports similar conclusions: "Nibbana is purely and solely an ethical state, to be reached in this birth by ethical practices, contemplation and insight. It is therefore not transcendental. . . . Expressions which deal with the realization of emancipation from lust, hatred, and illusion apply to practical habits and not to speculative thought."[29] Mr. Rhys-Davids personally had little patience with talk of karma and rebirth. In his interpretation of nirvana he emphasized its this-worldly significance, and in doing so undoubtedly came closer to the antispeculative attitude of the Buddha himself.

Nor is the ethical interpretation of nirvana limited to nineteenth century scholars. Twentieth century positivism gave training and fuel to empiricist interpreters of Buddhism who read the Pali Canon after their own leanings, rejecting all transcendental tinges.

Roy Amore, known for his attempts to trace Buddhist influence in the Christian gospels, is one who holds this view. Amore quotes from the *Samyutta Nikāya* with evident approval, contending that:

> Buddhist thought more commonly employs the straightforward statement that Nirvāna is the extinction of the three evil root causes [deep-seated mental complexes]: lust, hatred, and delusion. Once a wandering ascetic questioned the learned disciple Sariputta as follows . . . "Tell me sir, just what is this nirvāna?" "Sire [*sic*], the destruction of lust, hatred, and delusion is what is called nirvāna".[30]

Amore adduces further quotations from Sri Lankan monks to confirm his viewpoint, although their transcendentalist leanings are not easily concealed.[31]

David Kalupahana is another whose radical empiricism has won him fame for his unique interpretations of early Buddhism. He claims to be carrying out the intentions of his teacher Jayatilleke, who he feels has betrayed his own principles and "undermined the whole basis of Buddhist empiricism" by his admission of transempirical states after death.[32] Kalupahana insists that nirvana is a state to be found only within the experience of this life: "It is a state of perfect mental health (*aroga*), of perfect happiness (*parama sukha*), calmness or coolness (*sītibhūta*), and stability (*anenja*), etc. attained in this life, or while one is alive."[33] While insisting that the Buddha was silent because there is no way of knowing about transempirical states after death, Kalupahana seems to deny the possibility of such states in his positivist empiricist premises.

Japanese Mahayana Buddhists also tend to emphasize the ethical implications of nirvana in this life, which they prefer to term *satori* (enlightenment). In Mahayana Buddhism the ethical state of the enlightened person is not merely one of apathy nor of total detachment; it is one of action and compassion as well. It closely follows the *Bhagavad Gita*'s model of selfless action (*niskamkarma*) and makes way for the model of the Bodhisattva: the compassionate enlightened being who returns to this suffering world to save and help unenlightened sentient beings. Yamakami explains: "In its negative aspect, Nirvana is the extinction of the three-fold fires of lust, malice, and folly. . . . In its positive aspect, Nirvana consists in the practice of the three cardinal virtues of generosity, love, and wisdom."[34]

D. T. Suzuki denies that non-Buddhists are even qualified to deal with the problem of nirvana, but his own interpretation appears very similar to Yamakami's. For Suzuki, nirvana is destruction "of the notion of ego-substance and of all the desires that arise from this erroneous conception. But this represents the negative side of the doctrine, and its positive side consists in universal love or sympathy (*karuna*) for all beings."[35]

Many scholars of stature have thus interpreted nirvana as a state purely limited to the world of the living with little or no reference to existence after death. Some interpret nirvana as mere detachment from worldly desires, others add the requirement of positive ethical action within the world. While this may seem to be a more noncommittal and hence safer approach than the extremes of nihilism or eternalism, it still tends either to one side or the other.

If this line of thinking denies altogether that the Buddha was concerned with life after death, then the whole cycle of existence of karma and rebirth is rendered meaningless and unimportant. If the entire message of the Buddha were simply that people should be moral and not concern themselves with the afterlife, then no matter how profound this philosophical attitude it lacks the conviction of one who has seen that people are reborn repeatedly into lives of suffering and that all karma must bear fruit. If simply being detached or compassionate in itself is enough to eliminate suffering and karma, we should expect some further description of how such actions or attitudes stop the cycles of birth, death, and rebirth that are the bottom line of Buddhist philosophy.

Most ethical state interpreters of nirvana tend to indicate that for the enlightened person there is no life after death worth worrying about. This is clearly Suzuki's attitude, and is also noticeable in the other writers mentioned. But if there is no life whatsoever after death, then we are led again into the camp of the annihilationists, which we have already seen is inappropriate. By shifting the emphasis to the this-worldly realm of ethics the interpreters just discussed above have changed the focus of Buddhism from ontology to axiology. They seem, by their silence, to avoid some of the criticisms that were leveled against early annihilationist views, and wrongly against the Buddha himself. For the purposes of our study, however, they either fail to provide any answer to the question "Is nirvana a state surviving death?" or else they provide an annihilationist answer, which we have already shown to be unacceptable to the Buddha himself. Thus the question remains: Can there be a state after death compatible with the Buddha's teachings that avoids the eternal soul doctrine?

A Selfless State of Postmortem Existence

We have already seen that early Buddhism makes reference to two types of nirvana: sopadhisesa ("with remnant") and nirupadhisesa ("without remnant"). The former is the state of the saint still living in the world, the latter is the state of the saint after death. Even if we admitted that the ethical state interpretation adequately explained the meaning of extinction (in terms of extinction of desires while the body still lives), we would still be left with the troubling question of what is meant by a bodiless ethical state; the second kind of nirvana discussed.

It makes no sense to speak of postmortem apathy, detachment, or compassion in a being that ceases to exist after death. Moreover, we have already seen that the Buddha repudiated nihilism and affirmed that he would continue to exist. We also know that nirvana does not refer to a personal, body-dependent existence after death, for the body and khandhās are held to separate. And Buddhism clearly repudiates the notion of permanent or unchanging entities, including souls, in this material phenomenal universe. As in Conan Doyle's famous phrase, when all else is ruled impossible, the improbable must remain the fact.

So it seems with early Buddhism: both eternalism and annihilationism have been ruled impossible, and nirvana must mean something more than an ethical state since there is a type of nirvana after the body is dead and inactive. However distasteful to our language-bound Western thought patterns, the only alternative seems to be an extant state that language does not adequately describe, and yet which the Buddha and *arhats* experienced before and after death. This state, although difficult to characterize or talk about, is not nothing—it is nirvana.

How can we describe the ever-changing nature of the phenomenal world and the similarity-in-difference of the person who is reborn with the person who has died? Buddhists often use the analogies of a flame passing from wick to wick and ultimately extinguished, or of different water always flowing through the "same" river. Indeed, the analogy of the flame seems especially appropriate in expressing the burning, fleeting nature of the passions that leap from one object to another and are eventually extinguished. But extinction of the flame is not the only analogy for nirvana. Another important one is that of the small flame swallowed up in a larger one. As King Menander learns from monk Nāgasena:

> "Reverend Nāgasena," said the King, "does the Buddha still exist?"
> "Yes, your majesty, he does."

"Then is it possible to point out the Buddha as being here or there?" . . .

"If a great fire were blazing, would it be possible to point to a flame which had gone out and say that it was here or there?"[36]

Thus, there is a sense in which the individual flame is no longer identifiable, no longer individual, no longer limited to a single wick. The flame is not necessarily destroyed, but may actually be expanded by losing its prior individuality. It is rather like raindrops falling into the ocean: they do not lose all existence whatsoever, but rather lose the prior limitations and characteristics of their separateness. Of course, all such materialistic analogies have serious drawbacks in expressing states of consciousness. Pande concludes: "[Nirvāna] takes away the sting of death and leads to immortality in the sense of the 'Upasama' [merging] of the individual in a higher reality, like that of a burning flame in its source."[37]

Narasu also insists that "the denial of a separate self, an *ātman*, does not obliterate the personality of a man, but liberates the individual from an error."[38] This may seem like a very foreign concept to individualistically indoctrinated Westerners. How can we reconcile this view of a world of peace and bliss, a nirvana of no birth, death, nor change, with the Buddhist dictum that *all* is change and suffering?

Conze answers that the rules of change and suffering apply to this phenomenal world, but that nirvana refers to a noumenal, ultimate reality which stands beyond the pale of "the sensory world of illusion and ignorance, a world inextricably interwoven with craving and greed."[39] Conze feels that the realm of nirvana is a realm akin to that which Western mystics also have so much trouble describing, and which can be reached in one's own experience only by long meditative discipline. Sarathchandra similarly insists: "In the state of *nibbāna*, considered both as an objective sphere beyond that of the world of matter, as well as subjectively as a state reached by meditation, the individual attains final release from transmigration in the world of gods and men."[40]

There is a famous passage in which the Buddha asserts that there is a state which is unborn and uncompound.[41] This reference also proposes that nirvana *is*, that the Buddha who has attained nirvana *is*, and that this teaching is not merely a sugar coating for a doctrine of annihilationism. Why, then, was the Buddha so adamantly silent about the nature of this state? Pande suggests that "One describes it best by preserving silence, for to say anything about it would be to make it relational and finite. . . . Buddha adhered to this position so rigorously that his silence has become enigmatic."[42]

Thomas concludes that the Buddha had reached the realization of a state about which neither existence nor nonexistence as we know it could be asserted. LaVallée Poussin agrees that Western language lacks the subtlety needed to convey the nature of nirvanic states. If Conze is correct that only mystical knowledge is possible of nirvana, then it is understandable that the Buddha should desire to avoid easily misinterpreted metaphors. Jayatilleke reasons that "the person who has attained the goal is beyond measure (*na pamanam atthi*). Elsewhere, it is said that he does not come within time, being beyond time (*kappam neti akappiyo*) or that he does·not come within reckoning (*na upeti sankham*). In other words, we do not have the concepts or words to describe adequately the state of the emancipated person."[43] It is just this inaccessibility to verbal description that has rendered nirvana such a difficult concept for language-bound Western philosophers.

The negative adjectives which are so often applied to nirvana should not be taken as evidence of Buddhist nihilism. Instead, like the *via negativa* of the medieval Christian descriptions of the mystic Holy, these negative descriptions deny that nirvana has anything in common with the mundane or conceptual. Upadhyaya explains, "They by denying everything mundane and conceptual to Nibbāna suggest its supramundane and non-conceptual nature in the best possible way, though the positive expressions are also useful in so far as they assert the reality of Nibbāna and allay the fears of the nihilistic conception."[44]

With typical Buddhist logic, we are left with this conclusion: Nirvana neither exists nor does not exist, i.e., it is neither within the realm of existence as we know it, nor is it an illusion. The saint is not reborn, nor does he die, nor is it proper to use any ordinary adjectives about the ineffable state he experiences. His old personality does not continue, and yet the person is not utterly annihilated. Such a state of nirvana is achievable, and it is a viable alternative to rebirth after death.

Those relying on Aristotelian two-valued logic may dislike this approach. However, it is important to recognize that nirvana is not a purely theoretical and unfalsifiable entity, but a goal which the Buddha invites every man to try to find and experience for himself. (This is not sexist language. Women invited themselves into the monastic community later with the Buddha's begrudging permission; the Buddha did not originally invite women to meditate or become monks.)

Christians may fear the loss of personal identity in the absorption into the ultimately real. Here we can only observe that some great Christian mystics have shared this vision and these figures of speech. Nor is there anything inherently preferable in the Christian view that a person's individuality is of paramount importance, over the Buddhist view that personal individuality is the source of personal suffering.

To accept that there are states of being that are beyond the phenomenal and that are not even amenable to description in everyday discourse may require a radical change of worldview for Westerners lacking in mystical experience. Yet the idea that there are blissful but otherwise indescribable nirvanic states is the clearest conclusion we can reach concerning what the Buddha experienced and was trying to communicate. Even the Buddha, who had tasted nirvana in this life, realized the ineffability of his attainment. He called it "profound, difficult to comprehend, tranquil, subtle, beyond reason, excellent, realizable by the wise."[45] His interpreters, both Indian and Western, have struggled with various nihilist and eternalist versions of nirvana, and we have seen that neither is necessary.

Buddhism presents us with two alternatives to the Western ideas of survival in heavenly realms: (1) a rebirth of mental processes and characteristics into another human or nonhuman body; (2) an achievement of a transcendent bodiless state defying further referential description but characterizable by peace, bliss, and the absence of change and desire. Whether these theories can be empirically tested will be the burden of a later section of this book, but we have seen that rebirth and nirvana are viable concepts, at least within the Buddhists' logical systems. Because of the drastic difference between the logic, assumptions, empiricism, and worldviews of Buddhists and modern materialists, we should be wary of a linguistic analysis in English alone, or positivistic demands for visible referents in order to make sense of language.

However, nirvana was to be reached through the meditation and moral living of individual men. (Buddhists held that neither women nor animals could aspire to nirvana.) Nirvana could be attained only by an individual's long and devoted practice of meditation. This seemed to lead to a self-centering, a concern by the individual for the individual's own salvation (nirvana), in virtual disregard of the salvation of anyone else. Ironically, this self-centeredness was precisely what the Buddha was trying to avoid by his anattā theory, but Theravāda monks fell prey to this same criticism of self-centered salvation.

Later Buddhists came to become increasingly concerned with the salvation of all sentient beings and not just of the meditators themselves. This led them to develop a branch of Buddhism called Mahayana, or "The Greater Vehicle." This contrasted with the Theravāda, which they prejudicially called Hīnayāna, or "The Lesser Vehicle." In their pursuit of a less self-centered and more universalistic version of a path to nirvana, Mahaya-nists came to develop new visions of the afterlife, most promi-nent of which was the heavenlike Pure Land.

3

The Afterlife
in Pure Land
Buddhism

WE HAVE OBSERVED that early Buddhism offered two post-mortem alternatives: either continued samsara, rebirth and suffering, or nirvana. Both of these conditions deny the permanence of the self or a soul-like entity. Within the first thousand years after the Buddha's passing, however, there arose many Mahayana Buddhist sects with radically different interpretations of life after death. This chapter traces the history of the Mahayana ideas of *Buddha fields* (*Buddhaksetra*) and notes where these other worlds fit within the Mahayana Buddhist ontology. Later chapters investigate Pure Land epistemology, including the ways in which Pure Land Buddhists claimed to know the nature of Buddha fields.

To limit our scope, we shall take the philosophy of Pure

Land Buddhism as the prime example of Buddhist depictions of otherworldly heavens. While Pure Land Buddhism was neither a single school nor extricable from its connections with other sects, it did have distinctly identifiable features and sources. Our accounts of Pure Land ontology and epistemology are distilled from the three Pure Land sutras and from the writings of the major figures of the Pure Land tradition in China and Japan. We shall also look briefly at the experiential evidence on the nature of life after death in the Pure Land tradition.

Mahayana Buddhists made sense of personal survival in heavenly realms invisible to this world. In their search for logical consistency and practical verificaton principles, early Pure Land Buddhists were as rigorous as today's philosophers and scientists. After studying their system, we shall be better able to evaluate its philosophical viability, to resolve the issue of its foreign borrowings, and to advance our understanding of the alternatives possible in personal survival of death in a Mahayana Buddhist context.

The Mahayana Idea of Merit Transference

Early Buddhism taught a monastic lifestyle midway between the extremes of self-mortification and hedonism, emphasizing mental discipline and insight as well as physical self-control. The India in which early Buddhism was born already contained a plethora of religious philosophies. Among the most important of these were priestly hierarchies that practiced ritual sacrifices following the Vedas for the benefit of military and political patrons. The Buddha's teachings, however, seemed to offer liberation only to the individual who could devote his entire life to religious practices. It is not surprising to find that traditional priests criticized the Buddhist teachings as inferior to rituals that benefited many people simultaneously.[1]

From its Hindu contemporaries and later from evangelical

Christian missionaries, Theravada Buddhism faced charges of atheism and self-centeredness. Yet not long after its inception, the seeds of a theology of compassion and altruism were already evident. At one point in the classical text *Kuddhakapatha*, it is suggested that heavenly rebirth and even nirvana may be obtained through accumulation of merit.[2] In the *Kathāvatthu*, we find a debate about the production of merit by making gifts to departed spirits (Sanskrit: *pretas*).[3] By the time of the *Milinda-panha*, the idea that a surplus of merit can be shared with or transferred to the departed is fairly well established.[4] If suffering spirits can benefit from human compassion, then analogously, suffering humans also might benefit from the compassion of beings still higher on the "chain of being" such as deceased arhats or *bodhisattvas*.

Such Mahayanist ideas took ready root in Chinese soil. The Chinese had long believed that their ancestors benefited from offerings made by their living descendants.[5] Funeral practices were designed to assist the souls of the departed,[6] and there was a growing pre-Buddhist literature about dead men who visited heaven and later returned to earth.[7] The Chinese mind did not separate this world from the next as consciously as do modern thinkers. Giving food or even merit from one realm to another was like sending gifts or praise from one earthly kingdom to another. The origins of the central Mahayana doctrine of merit transference can thus be found in both pre-Buddhist Hindu and Chinese societies.

Bodhisattvas

The early Buddhist concept of nirvana was that of a state transcending all realms of birth and death, causality, time, and change. This idea was grounded in the meditative experiences and insights of the Buddha himself. Although the Buddha asked his disciples to try it for themselves, the disciplined path of the

Buddha was not open to the average person. Nor were the imageless descriptions of selflessness and quiescent beatitude designed to capture the minds of the multitudes. The terms used to characterize nirvana in a positive way were attractive enough to be sure (peace, bliss, coolness, calmness), but they lacked any sensual imagery. To make these qualities of nirvana more understandable and desirable, they were first analogized to physical pleasures like the coolness of water or the light of the sun. Gradually the notion arose that paradisiacal lands actually existed in which these nirvanic qualities were embodied and experienceable, "fostered by people's need for a concrete realm in which to look forward to being reborn, and by the growing desire to worship Buddha and be with him in person."[8]

Along with the gradual deificaton of the Buddha came the growth of the bodhisattva idea. For the Buddha had declared that all men could test his path for themselves, implying that others could achieve similar spiritual insights by their own efforts. Admittedly, no other Buddhas were on the horizon at the time. But the Indian worldview envisioned vast expanses of cosmic time and vast stretches of outer space. Surely there were other realms in which other beings had reached enlightenment after *kalpas* (cosmic eons) of discipline and self-perfection. In their perfected powers and wisdom, these enlightened bodhisattvas could see humans and reach out compassionately towards them. While time and space might prevent common people from perceiving them, that did not mean that they did not exist.

Just as the Buddha had been surrounded by attentive disciples and arhats during his lifetime, the Mahayanists developed the image that now the Buddha (who had not died but passed into nirvana) was surrounded by bodhisattvas. These bodhisattvas remained in a near-nirvanic state, continually listening to his blessed *dharma* (teachings of truth). The precise ontological status of this realm, somewhere between samsara and the nirvana of nondistinction, became a problem (like that of heaven in Christianity) that we shall examine in detail later. At the moment, we should try to understand the historic origins and development of the idea of bodhisattvas and their heavenlike Buddha fields.

Even in early Buddhism, the concept of a dharma-propagating world monarch, who also bears the marks of a Buddha, is found in the canonical *Dīgha Nikāya*.[9] The *Samyutta Nikāya* explains how Sakka, the king of the gods, attained his position through long ethical disciplines. These accounts may well serve as forerunners or models of the early bodhisattva concept; Rowell finds this influence of the *cakravartin* (world ruler) model particularly compelling.[10] So we can trace the roots of the bodhisattvas to a combination of factors: the idea of merit transference, the idea that enlightened beings survive death in a near-nirvanic state, and the idea of divine kings.

Buddha Fields

While many arhats or bodhisattvas might conceivably surround the Buddha, the scriptures made it clear that there was only one Buddha within any given world system.[11] At the same time, there was a growing tendency in Buddhism to expand the conception of the universe from that of a single network to that of millions of universes, either infinitely distant from each other or as interpenetrating systems.

> Cosmological discussions soon found their way into Buddhism, and their picture of the make-up of the total cosmos soon outreached the paltry ten-thousand-world systems which seem to have stood for the whole universe in the time of the earlier *Nikāyas* . . . . Just as this world has its Buddha Sakyamuni and constitutes his field, so (when the cosmos had expanded to include many sets of world-systems) each of the myriad other universes has its own Buddha and constitutes his field.[12]

Fujita finds four external influences that may have encouraged the development of the concept of Buddha lands: the idea of the universal monarch and descriptions of his mythological kingdom of *Kusavati*; stories of the northern land of Kuru around Mt. Meru; tales of the Hindu heavens; and the worship of *stupas* (originally burial mounds of the saints, which became embellished into ornate temples, the centers of much pomp and ceremony).[13] He finds the myths of the Hindu heavens especially analogous to those of the Buddha lands, both in their development of visual imagery to depict an invisible realm of principle (brahman or dharma) and in the specific contents of the Buddha realms (*Brahmaloka*) and Buddha fields (*Buddhaksetra*), following Nakamura.[14]

In short, by the time of the Christian era, five centuries after the passing of the Buddha, Buddhism had undergone numerous major theoretical adaptations. Some were in an effort to relate to or compete with contemporary Indian religions, and others were part of a maturation process that demanded compassion, visual imagery, and attainable salvation. These factors resulted in the doctrines of transference of merit, of compassionate bodhisattvas, and of many simultaneous heavenly Buddha lands.

By the second century of the Christian era, numerous competing Buddhist sects had each developed their own versions of blessed Buddha fields that could be attained at death in reward for any number of meritorious practices. Transcendent heavens had become such a common feature of Buddhist literature that the name *Sukhāvatī*, which originally referred only to the land created by *Amitābha* bodhisattva, became used as a general term for anything heavenly.[15]

By the time Buddhism encountered China, it was neither a self-centered asceticism nor an antimetaphysical empiricism. It included concrete images of godlike bodhisattvas who compassionately reached across whole world systems to help their devotees, and layers of heavenly Buddha lands intermediate between this realm of rebirth (samsara) and the ultimate realm of selflessness (nirvana). Pure Land Buddhist philosophy is the paradigmatic example of a well developed Mahayana view of the afterlife.

Descriptions of the Pure Land

Scriptural authority for the Pure Land of Amida is found in the *Larger* and *Smaller Pure Land Sutras* (*Sukhāvati-vyūha Sūtras*) of which Sanskrit,Tibetan, and Chinese versions are available. There is some debate about precise dates, but scholars tend to place the first Chinese translations in the third century A.D., suggesting that the Sanskrit originals might have been composed a century or two before that date.[16] A third scriptural source, the *Meditation on Amida Sutra* (*Amitāyur-dhyāna Sūtra*), lacks pre-Chinese equivalents and does not appear until perhaps 440 A.D.[17] The *Gāthā on the Larger Sutra*, attributed to Vasubandhu,[18] and the writings of T'an-luan, Tao-ch'o, and Shan-tao are also treated with almost scriptural authority by modern Pure Land Buddhists. Minor differences in these scriptures give rise to factionalism in the Japanese context, but the descriptions of the Pure Land in each of the sutra sources are generally in agreement.

Access to the Pure Land

The *Larger Sutra* tells the story of Dharmakara, who lived lives analogous to those attributed to Gautama Siddhartha, renouncing luxury to work for many kalpas (eons) of meditation and self-sacrifice in order to become a bodhisattva. Before Lokesvarāja, the lord of the universe, he vowed to save all beings in a pure Buddha land. Dharmakara determined to use his store of merit and meditative powers of image projection to create a Pure Land at the completion of his endeavors. His vows describe the perfections of that land, the beings in it, and the methods by which humans can reach his land.

Each vow concludes with the prayer, or vow, "if I fail in this . . . may I not attain enlightenment." It is a premise of the sutra that Dharmakara has already completed his practice, and now rules the Pure Land as Amida. Therefore, the descriptions of heaven and the conditions of salvation are also taken to be established. The bodhisattva who is speaking in this passage about the means to reach his Buddha land is alternately referred to as *Amitāyus* (the Buddha of limitless life) and *Amitābha* (the Buddha of limitless light), both of which are implied by the abbreviated form *Amida*. The conditions necessary for birth in the Pure Land are epitomized by the eighteenth, nineteenth, and twentieth vows, which may be summarized as follows:

18. All beings in ten directions with sincere profound faith who seek to be born in my land and call upon my name ten times, except those who have committed the five cardinal crimes or injured the true dharma, shall be born in my land.
19. I will appear at the moment of death to all beings of the ten directions committed to enlightenment and the practice of good deeds, who seek to be born in my land.
20. All beings of the ten directions who hear my name, desire the Pure Land, and practice virtue in order to attain the Pure Land will succeed.[19]

The land which Amida has established and over which he presides is also characterized by radiance and light. Its trees, ponds, fields, and palaces glow like precious metals and gemstones. The ground is covered with flowers that perfume the gentle breezes, and the birds and trees make soft harmonious music. Surrounded by bodhisattvic disciples in the center of all this harmony is the huge golden figure of Amida himself, preaching the dharma. There are no impurities: no ghosts, beasts, nor women. There is no sickness nor death; food is abundant but unnecessary.[20] There are no rules and no conflicts;

free will is universal. But since cravings have been eliminated and everyone's wills are in accord with the dharma, there is no sin.[21] This Pure Land is a unique state intermediate between samsara and nirvana from which attainment of nirvana is ultimately guaranteed.

Wish Fulfillment

Another unique feature of the Pure Land of Amida is that the environment of the Pure Land is said to conform itself to the (nonconflicting) wills or wishes of the individuals therein. Many interesting specific examples are given. The twenty-fourth vow (twenty-second vow in Sanskrit versions) promises that if the beings dwelling in the Pure Land wish their store of merit to metamorphize into any beautiful perceptible form, it will appear before them immediately. Later it continues:

> Again, O Ananda, the borders of those great rivers on both sides are filled with jewel trees of various scents, from which bunches of flowers, leaves, and branches of all kinds hang down. And if the beings who are on the borders of those rivers wish to enjoy sport full of heavenly delights, the water rises to the ankle only after they have stepped into the rivers, if they wish it to be so; or if they wish it, the water rises to their knees, to their hips, to their sides, and to their ears. And heavenly pleasures arise. Again, if the beings then wish the water to be cold, it is cold; if they wish it to be hot, it is hot; if they wish it to be hot and cold, it is hot and cold according to their pleasure.[22]

Similarly, it is related that those who wish to hear music, or the dharma, or some sermon, hear it as soon as they wish it. Those who do not wish to hear, hear nothing at that time. Those who wish to smell any fragrance have merely to think on it, and it wafts to their noses, while those who wish for different (or no) fragrances smell according to their desires.

There is apparently a contradiction here, for how could two

people in the same place have very different sensations of sounds or smells? The *Larger Sutra* makes clear that this is possible precisely because it is an idealistic realm (like that explained by Bishop Berkeley). Neither the bodies of the perceivers nor the objects of their perceptions are objectively external, rather, all reality is a projection of mental images.

> And again, O Ananda, in that world Sukhāvatī, beings do not take food consisting of gross materials such as gravy or molasses, but whatever food they desire, such food they perceive, as if it were taken, and become delighted in body and mind. Yet they need not put it into their mouths. . . . If they desire cloaks of different colors and many hundred thousand colors, then with these very best cloaks, the whole Buddha country shines. And the people feel themselves covered. . . . And if they desire such ornaments, jewels . . . they perceive themselves to be adorned with these ornaments. . . . And if they desire a palace, with colors and emblems . . . exactly such a palace appears. [23]

The collective or objective features of the Pure Land are those generated by Amida's transcendent mind; its will-dependent or subjective features are those projected by the minds of the individual perceivers. Since there are only perceptions and no physical objects, one person's desires and perceptions need not infringe on any other's. This unique correspondence of the Buddha land to the wishes of its inhabitants is the final characteristic of the Pure Land listed in Vasubandhu's description; it is similarly noted and praised by contemporary Master Hua in his exposition of the *Smaller Sutra*.[24]

The Solipsistic Calyx State

There is nothing explicitly purgatorial about the Pure Land. It is seen as a waiting stage or intermediate state ideally suited for the meditation and practice conducive to the attainment of nirvana. There is a curious provisional state, however, for those who are born into the Pure Land by their own merits and by hearing the dharma but who "doubt the knowledge of the Buddha."[25] The faithful are born full grown from lotuses in the ponds of the Pure Land (there is no sexual reproduction). But the doubters are born into the dark tubular calyxes of the lotuses where they exist in (spiritual) darkness, hidden from the light of Buddha and dharma.

These doubters are still free from all disagreeable and painful experience. They are conscious of all comforts. They too can experience palaces and gardens, but theirs is a totally subjective idealistic realm. They are analogized to a king imprisoned alone in his own luxurious palace. Their punishment is that they cannot escape, cannot hear the dharma, cannot amass more moral merit nor progress spiritward for a period of 500 years. So they soon lose all satisfaction in their illusory pleasures and come to desire only their full birth into the presence of Amida Buddha and consequent knowledge of the dharma. Pure Land Master T'an-luan (d. ca. 554 A.D.) comments:

> Although they dwell in seven jewelled palaces, and have fine objects, smells, tastes, and sensations, yet they do not regard this as pleasure. Rather they regard it as suffering that they do not see the Three Precious Ones [Buddha, Dharma, Sangha] and that they cannot revere them and practice all of the various kinds of good deeds. They recognize their basic transgressions, and deeply repenting them, seek only to leave that place."[26]

The Ontology of the Pure Land

Levels of Existence

If we are to understand the nature of the Pure Land, we must place it in the context of the Mahayana view of the universe. The entire realm of samsara—of birth and death, causal conditioning, impermanence and suffering—is believed to consist of three worlds: the world of desire (this world), the world of form, and the world beyond form. The latter two worlds are heavenly realms inhabited only by gods and accessible only through meditation or rebirth; they are rarefied planes devoid of matter, and they are so rarely experienced that they are little discussed.

The world of desire, lowest on the continuum, consists of six paths or levels (*gati*) comprised of gross (visible) and subtle (invisible) matter ranging from hell-dwellers, ghosts, and animals to titans, humans, and desire-ridden gods. Although ultimately unreal in the sense that it will be transcended, this material realm seems to possess a physical nature independent of our perceptions of it, and seems relatively impervious to merely mental attempts to change it. The Buddha born into this realm is called the *nirmānakāya*, or transformation body.

In traditional Buddhism, the only alternative to this samsara was nirvana, which underlies and transcends all change and distinctions. Characterized positively, it is a realm of pure bliss and truth; negatively described, it is pure void, the realization of the illusoriness of all else. The Buddha eternally exists at this level, but has a body of truth (*dharmakāya*) only in a metaphoric and not in a physical or perceptible sense. Somewhere between samsara and nirvana must lie the Pure Land. (Sects differ as to whether this is within or beyond the three worlds.) The Pure Land is neither subject to change and suffering nor is it identifiable with nirvana itself. We can tentatively outline the situation as follows:[27]

I. Dharma-realm: Noumenon, expressing the *dharmakāya* of Buddha. This realm is not only above, but underlying and interpenetrating all levels; the supersensible ground of all.

II. Recompense realm: from merit accumulation in the Triple World. Also called the Response realm, emanating from the higher Dharma realm for the sake of responding to the needs of beings. Into this realm is expressed the Reward Body or Compensation Body (*sambhogakāya*) of Amida and other transcendent bodhisattvas. It includes the intersubjective idealism of the Pure Land and the subjective idealisms of the calyx states.

III. Transformation realm, in which the *nirmānakāya* is manifest. Called the Triple World, it may be subdivided into:

A. World of no form (*arūpadhātu*), including four heavens corresponding to the fifth through eighth *bhūmis* (meditative stages).

B. World of form (*rūpadhātu*), including eighteen heavens; nine for the fourth bhūmi and three heavens each for the first, second, and third bhūmis.

C. World of desire (*kāmadhātu*) including six levels:

1. Six Heavens of Desire (*satkāmāvacarā*)
2. Humans (*manusya*)
3. Titans (*asura*)
4. Animals, including insects (*tiryag-yoni*)
5. Ghosts (*preta*)
6. Eight Hells (*naraka*)

The sutras themselves do not make explicit where the Pure Land of Amida falls within this Buddhist scheme, and this has naturally led to numerous interpretations. The most common anti-Pure Land objection was that if laymen could hope to reach the Western Pure Land by simple devotionalism, then it must lie within the realm of form like the heavens of the gods.[28] Others, like Ching-ying Hui-yuan, admitted that the Pure Land transcended heavens of desire and form but emphasized the shallowness of an idealistic land: "Although this land is pure, it is generated by erroneous thoughts and hence is as empty and unreal as what is seen in a dream."[29]

In fact, this criticism might apply appropriately to the calyx state where *all* experiences and impressions are the solipsistic product of the individual's mental activity. However, this fails to consider the objective idealism conferred on the major features of the Pure Land by Amida Buddha (acting in much the same role as God in Bishop Berkeley's idealism). It is true that even the perceptual forms of the Pure Land must at some point be overcome. It is not true that they are therefore unimportant, nor that they are materialistic just because they seem to have form to the perceivers.

Objective Idealism of the Pure Land

Those who are now accepted as the patriarchs of the Pure Land tradition are fairly unanimous in their placement of the Pure Land above samsara. Vasubandhu rhapsodizes, "When I meditate on the aspects of your land, they go beyond the way of the three worlds."[30]

T'an-luan takes a more careful and logical approach, arguing that:

1. Sukhāvatī has form, so it is not in the formless realm;
2. It has solidity and location, but rūpadhātu (the world of pure form) has no location nor solidity, so Sukhāvatī is not in rūpadhātu.
3. Sukhāvatī transcends desires, so is not in the world of desire.
4. So Sukhāvatī is not in or of the triple world of samsara.
5. We know from meditative experience that the Pure Land exists.
6. Therefore, its existence must be subtle and transcendental; outside of samsara, but not yet nirvana.

Corless observes, "The subtle existence of a realm outside the triple world is a key point in T'an-luan's thought."[31] T'an-luan adds that since the Pure Land is created by Amida's mind it has an objectivity and ontological status superior to the mental illusions which men create.[32]

Tao-ch'o is more explicit, stating that "Amida is the Recompensed Buddha (sambhogakāya), and that the land of bliss, adorned with gems, is the recompensed Land."[33] Tao-ch'o had to defend the aspiration for the Pure Land from critics who held that any notion of shapes, forms, lands, or gems was an unworthy ideal. Tao-ch'o found theoretical justification for seeking the Pure Land by an inversion of the Two Truths theory. In the *Vimalakīrtinirdesa Sūtra*, it is said that bodhisattvas, while knowing the lands of their creation to be noumenally unreal, are still justified in creating such illusions as the Pure Land to save sentient beings. Tao-ch'o takes this to mean that we humans are equally justified in discriminating and using these phenomenal forms for our own benefit, since this is in response to the bodhisattva's creation of the Pure Land.[34]

Of course, the use of phenomenal forms in the Pure Land is on a very sophisticated level (for the purpose of enlightenment and not sensual gratification), since there are no lusts nor nonspiritual interests in the Pure Land. Still, Tao-ch'o's interpretation of the Two Truths theory served to philosophically legitimize the concretization of nirvanic qualities into Pure Land imagery. This reinforced the idea that the Pure Land, although ultimately idealist and illusory, would nonetheless be experienced as a very real-seeming phenomenon after death.

There may seem to be a contrast between the relatively objective worlds of form and matter (invisible and visible) and the relatively subjective worlds of idea projection (response lands). Ultimately, these are variations only in degree of the percipients' delusion and not in underlying ontology. From an ultimate standpoint, even the most stubbornly objective realms of appearance are themselves mere productions of mind. This is made clear in numerous scriptural sources.

The *Karunā-pundarīka* relates a curious dialogue between

the Buddha and Mahābrahmā, in which the Buddha persuades Mahābrahmā that he had not created the world, and Mahābrahmā asks the Buddha for instruction. The Buddha responds: "It is by karma [mental action, volition, and conception] that the world has been created . . . made to appear; by karma that beings have been created; it is from karma, arising from karma as a cause that the distinctions of being come to be."[35] Since karma refers primarily to mental activity, the Buddha is saying it is mental activity that has produced the world. This is as Rowell has shown, relying on Abhidharma as well as Mahayana texts.[36]

The *Hua-Yen* (Sanskrit: *Avatamsaka*) *Sūtra* is even clearer in reinforcing that all Buddha lands arise from the mind, taking on any and all forms. All are phenomenally real in the sense that they are experienceable, but all are noumenally grounded in mind alone.[37]

There is a subtle but important philosophical shift in the meaning of the word karma taking place in these discussions. The early Buddhists felt that karma would lead people to be reborn in worlds causally suited to their past thoughts and actions; people would choose just the right wombs and environments so that their past karmas might come to fruition. Mahayana Buddhists, on the other hand, were now proposing that previous karma not only affected the choice of, but in some sense actually created the whole world into which people would be reborn.

The projections by both humans and bodhisattvas are analogized to the *siddhis* (psychic powers) demonstrated by yogins and meditators in both Buddhist and Yogic traditions. Ultimately, therefore, both the Pure Land (including Amida's sambhogakāya) and the triple worlds (including Gautama's nirmānakāya) are equally illusory projections of one underlying Buddha/dharma, and they are equally real-seeming to those trapped within perceptual or discriminatory perspectives.

Then how can we determine which experiences are fundamental, and which misguided? More critically, if we are caught up in this realm of materialist desires, how can we know of such idealistic Pure Lands, much less attain them? This line of questioning brings us to the indispensability of meditation.

4

Finding
the Pure Land
Oneself

Meditation in Theory and Practice

LIKE THE EARLY BUDDHISTS, the later Mahayana Buddhists considered themselves to be basing their philosophy on real experience, not on fantasy. In this sense they may equally be called empiricists—but without the mechanistic materialist presuppositions that have traditionally dominated modern Western empiricism. Pure Land Buddhists accepted the provisional reality of all experiences, including dreams, visions, and meditative states. In particular, their meditative experiences tended to shed doubt on the ultimacy of the realm of sense impression and its underlying objectivity. The verification of the existence and invesigation of the nature of the Pure Land was considered to be within the capacities of sincere Pure Land Buddhist practitioners. Meditative vision, a longstanding Buddhist practice for gaining true knowledge, is the first tool of Pure Land epistemology, and its origins stem from the scriptures themselves.

Objects of Meditation

The *Meditation on Amitāyus Sutra* is a veritable handbook of the procedures to be followed in order to gain a vision of Amida. It begins by describing meditations on physical objects such as the setting sun or a bowl of water. The meditator is told to fix the objects permanently in his mind, so that he can realistically visualize them even with his eyes closed. This process, which we have called meditation, is not a discursive thinking about these things, but an envisioning, an imaging so clearly that the object of concentration actually seems to stand objective in its own right before the visualizer. Then the practitioner is told to hold this apparently externalized thought image steadfast and to inspect the image in minute visual detail.[1]

Following meditations on the sun, water, and physical objects, the *Meditation Sutra* tells the practitioner sequentially to visualize jewel trees, flowers, and then buildings of the Pure Land. Thereafter, he is to focus on the Buddha Amitāyus and his surrounding bodhisattvas in minute and attentive detail. As he focuses on each tiny part of the image or mark of the Buddha, it seems to expand and loom immense before him. Finally, he is told to meditate upon and realistically visualize his own rebirth in the Pure Land:

> Imagine thyself to be born in the World of Highest Happiness in the western quarter, and to be seated cross-legged, on a lotus flower there. Then . . . thine eyes will be opened so as to see the Buddhas and Bodhisattvas who fill the whole sky; thou wilt hear the sounds of waters and trees, the notes of birds, and the voices of many Buddhas preaching the excellent Law, in accordance with the twelve divisions of the scriptures. When thou hast

ceased from that meditation, thou must remember the experience ever after. . . . The innumerable incarnate bodies of Amitāyus, together with those of Avalokitesvara and Mahāsthāmaprāpta, constantly come and appear before such devotees [who have once achieved this meditation]."[2]

Although the *Meditation Sutra* does not detail the postures and preparations for meditation, much of this may be assumed to be known already by practicing Buddhists and therefore superfluous.

The Practice of Meditation

Among Chinese meditators, Shan-tao is the clearest in discussing the practical aspects of Pure Land meditation. To obtain such visions of the Pure Land, he says, one should ritually purify himself, limit his diet to small amounts of rice and vegetables, control his mind, repeat tens of thousands of mantras, and go without sleep for seven days(!).[3] In another context, he declares that confessions of one's sins should leave the practitioner crying streams of tears (an emotional catharsis) preparatory to these meditations.[4]

Pure Land meditations were also an important part of Tendai practice adopted by Saichō and Ennin (Jikaku), the monks who established Japanese Tendai Buddhism on Japan's Mt. Hiei after studying in China in the ninth century. Genshin (Eshin) (947–1017?) is among the Tendai masters who remain famous today for their emphasis on Pure Land meditation. He describes their "constantly walking meditation" in the following terms:

> For a single period of ninety days only circumambulate exclusively. . . . You should make this vow: "Even if my bones should wither and rot, I will not rest until I realize this samadhi." If you arouse the great faith, nothing can equal you; no one can rival the wisdom which you will enter into. Thus always obey your teacher. Until the three months have elapsed, have no worldly

desires even for the snap of a finger. Until the three months have elapsed, do not lie down even for the snap of a finger. Until the three months have elapsed, constantly walk without stopping [except for natural functions].[5]

In theory, then, the meditators of tenth-century Japanese Tendai Buddhism were not distant from their predecessors in China and even India. Both took vegetarianism, abstinence, and long, steady, devoted effort to be the minimal prerequisites for visions of the Pure Land.

Modern medical studies have shown that practices of sensory deprivation, sleeplessness, or emotional catharses alone are enough to produce visions. In Pure Land Buddhism these practices were taken together with incessant mantra repetitions and the conscious desire to project images of heavens or Buddhas. There can be little doubt that such visions were experienced as reported by some practitioners.

The critical difference, of course, is that modern medics would tend to interpret such experiences as nonreferential hallucinations of an unbalanced and disease-prone mind. This is based on their presupposition that the material world as perceived is the only normal and "real" standpoint. Buddhists, however, would say that it is precisely such meditative experiences which give the lie to the modern materialists' assumptions, and demonstrate that there are in fact other levels or layers to reality, which is itself ultimately mind dependent.

Evidence of Meditative Visions

Although not directly connected to the later Pure Land tradition, an early development in Chinese Pure Land meditation and practice was the establishment of the White Lotus group on Mount Lu-Shan by Hui-yuan in 402.[6] Hui-yuan himself was both interested in and personally prone to having visions of the Pure Land. He encouraged both meditation and the painting of imagery conducive to visualization by his followers. He was frequently ill in his later years, but his writings about the subtle powers of the soul as it moved detached from individual bodies are very reminiscent of accounts of modern out-of-body experiences.[7]

Visions were widely reported among his disciples as well. Liu Ch'eng-chih, who helped draft the charter of the White Lotus Society, saw images of the Buddha floating in the air around him after his meditations (as the *Meditation Sutra* had predicted). He also predicted the date of his own funeral, and passed away sitting upright and facing west without a trace of disease.[8]

Even devout Buddhists did not accept such experiences uncritically. Hui-yuan himself was troubled about the ontological status of such visions and sent many questions to Kumārajīva to clarify the matter.[9] We have already observed that Tao-ch'o felt that the observable forms of Amida and the Pure Land were created by the bodhisattva for our benefit, and thus were as provisionally real and useful as any other objects. His disciple Shan-tao strongly supported this claim.[10]

Shan-tao too had many impressive visualization experiences which inspired his art, his teaching, and his life.[11] He encountered the Pure Land in repeated trance experiences that he attempted to communicate through sermon and sculpture. He was so convincing that at least one listener promptly committed suicide in the hopes of attaining the Pure Land.[12] Master Fa-chao, often called the "second Shan-tao," had a vision of his master-to-be (Cheng-yuan) while meditating on the Pure Land, and promptly sought him out.[13] Fa-chao also had numerous visions while in constantly-walking meditation, and felt that he had been taught a five-tone mantra recitation by Amida himself.[14] It was this same Fa-chao who became the teacher of Ennin (who was visiting from Japan), who in turn conveyed the practices and teachings to Mt. Hiei.

We have already mentioned Genshin, whose *Essentials of Rebirth* (Japanese: *Ōjō Yōshū*) and paintings of hells and the

Pure Land gave a substantial impetus to Amida worship in Japan. The important thing to note about Genshin's paintings in this context is that they were inspired by vivid dreams and visions.[15] Rensei relates: "It was after his dreams that Eshin [Genshin] wrote the *Ōjō Yōshū*, and Chingai his *Ketsujō Ōjōshū*."[16] Also on Mt. Hiei, the Bishop Ryōnin, who had meditated for years in the Mudō-ji temple, changed his lifestyle and left to start the first Japanese Amidist sect after a vision: "In 1117, at the age of 46, Ryōnin experienced the most significant event in his life. . . . Amida appeared during his *nembutsu* meditation and directly revealed the philosophy of the *yūzū nembutsu* as the pathway to salvation. At the same time, he [Ryōnin] was presented with a visual mandala of Amida."[17]

Ryōnin thereupon went to the capital, converted the emperor, and had several visions of the god Bishamonten (Sanskrit: Vaisravana), in one of which he was presented a scroll "as proof of the heavenly visit."[18] The scroll no longer exists, but the interesting point is that no one protested about the interaction of the visionary world with the physical world in this way since both were accepted as being on some level illusory and ideational.

Gods also appeared to Ryōnin's disciple Eikū while he was praying,[19] and it was this same Eikū (along with Kōen, compiler of the *Fusō Ryakki*) who was to train the monk Genkū, better known as Hōnen. Hōnen emulated Shan-tao particularly because "Master Shan-tao embodied the virtue of *samādhi* [meditative vision]."[20] Hōnen also believed strongly in meditation, and in the first two months of 1148 alone he perfected the meditations on water, on the lapis lazuli land, and on the jewelled lakes, towers, and the lapis lazuli palace of the Pure Land.[21] So numerous and important were Hōnen's visions that he kept a careful record of them for eight years (1198–1206), with the notation that they were to be kept private until his death.[22]

It is interesting that Hōnen's greatest opponent and detractor, Kōben (Myōe), respected him throughout his life. It was only after the posthumous publication of Hōnen's *Senchakushū*, which advocates recitation over meditation, that Kōben attacked his position.[23] Kōben himself kept an elaborate record of his dreams for 40 years, "seemingly indicative of an inherent inclination to fall easily into *samādhi*, and also of his serious reverence for such experiences."

Although Kōben was of the Kegon school, his protest was not against the Pure Land. On the contrary, it was that Hōnen's advocacy of recitation over meditation strayed from true Pure Land practice.[24] Thus, even monks from other schools respected Pure Land meditation as a central practice that was key to verification of the scriptures. Pure Land Buddhists, however, had another chance to glimpse the Pure Land: the moment of death.

Deathbed Visions

Even in early Buddhism, the focus of consciousness at the moment of death was thought to have particular importance for the nature of rebirth.[25] While the Hindus envisioned karma as a supernatural storehouse of seeds waiting to bear fruit and the Jains depicted karma as invisible material dust clinging to the soul, the Buddhists thought of each moment as influencing subsequent moments in and through itself. It seemed probable that at their deaths bad men would harbor bad thoughts and good men noble thoughts, but there also seemed to be exceptions to this pattern.

The Buddha reported that in his enlightenment experience, he had seen bad men born into good situations and vice-versa, depending in part on the nature of their thoughts at the moments of their deaths.[26] When King Milinda asked how an evil person with sins as weighty as a stone could fail to fall into hell at death, it was explained that even a stone could float if placed in a boat.[27] In Pure Land Buddhism, the divine grace of Amida is analogized to this boat, which can save all beings regardless of the weight of their misdeeds if they simply trust in it. There are even some Hindu precedents for this idea, which was developed more thoroughly by later Vedantins.[28]

All three of the Pure Land sutras are predicated on the view that a person's consciousness at death can enable a rebirth into the Pure Land, through the miraculous power and aid of Amida. The *Larger Sutra* makes this explicit in the nineteenth (eighteenth vow in Sanskrit versions) vow:

> O Bhagavat, if those beings who have directed their thoughts towards the highest perfect knowledge in other worlds, and who, after having heard my name, when I have obtained the Bodhi [knowledge], have meditated on me with serene thoughts; if at the moment of their death, after having approached them, surrounded by an assembly of Bhiksus, I should not stand before them, worshipped by them, so their thoughts may not be troubled, then may I not obtain the highest perfect knowledge [which has already been obtained].[29]

We find a text of similar import in the *Smaller Sutra* as well:

> Whatever son or daughter of a family shall hear the name of the blessed Amitāyus, the Tathāgata, and having heard it, shall keep it in mind . . . when that son or daughter of a family comes to die, then that Amitāyus, the Tathāgata, surrounded by an assembly of disciples and followed by a host of Bodhisattvas, will stand before them at the hour of death, and they will depart this life with tranquil minds. After their death, they will be born in the world Sukhāvatī, in the Buddha country of the same Amitāyus . . . [30]

The *Meditation Sutra* goes into still more elaborate detail, describing how the deathbed experiences of people will differ according to the nature of their meditations and faith. Thus, the most accomplished of meditators sees Amida surrounded by countless bodhisattvas, his land and palace, and Amitāyus sends radiant light to shine upon the face of the dying believer. Those of lesser belief see flowers, thrones, and different colors of light according to their grades.

The lowest grades of people to be born into the Pure Land first briefly taste the fires of hell and then are rescued into flower-covered lakes. Or they may see a sunlike disc (without any retinues of bodhisattvas) to be followed by birth in the Pure Land forty-nine days (a short time) thereafter.[31] The important thing about these descriptions is that they tally with experiential accounts that have been recorded and preserved.

Deathbed Practices in Pure Land Buddhism

If we turn our attention to the best-known early cases in China, it is clear that Lu-shan Hui-yuan's White Lotus Society was not merely a meditational group, but was also a common compact to help each other achieve the Pure Land after death. Shan-tao, always an advocate of meditation, placed no lesser importance on the visions at the moment of death. He invoked his monks who attended the deathbeds of Pure Land believers:

> If the [dying] patient has a vision, let him tell the attendant about it. As soon as you have heard it, record it just as you have heard. Moreover, when the sick person is not able to relate it, the attendant should ask over and over, "What kind of vision do you see?" If he tells of seeing his sinful deeds, let those beside him reflect on the Buddha for him and assist him in his repentances and thoroughly cancel the sinful deeds. If the sinful deeds are canceled, and he sees before him in response to his Buddha-reflection the lotus dais holy assembly, record it just as described.[32]

The Japanese monk Genshin relates the above recommendation with evident approval. Clearly, Hōnen also felt that it was important to die composed in mind while continually reciting the name of Amida, to assure the vision of and passage to the Pure Land at death.[33]

While meditating monks first validated their religious faiths by their ascetic visualization practices and later found images of the Buddha spontaneously appearing in front of them, common believers were taught to expect Amida to meet them at their deathbeds if they were at peace with the cosmos.[34] Some later commentators have tried to interpret Pure Land Buddhism in a more existential and less soteriological sense, but this simply does not square with the clear meaning of the three central Pure Land scriptures. This interpretation is particularly unequivocal in the Chinese of T'an-luan.[35]

It was not until 1385 that Ryōyo (Shōgei) "wrought nothing short of a revolution" in Pure Land Buddhism by declaring that

> the ordinary conception of the soul's being transported to Paradise and born there was merely a figure of speech . . . the fact being that neither Amida, nor the sainted beings, nor the "nine ranks" are to be conceived as existing "over there" at all, because the Pure Land is the ultimate and absolute reality, and that is everywhere, so that we may be identified with it right here where we are.[36]

This interpretation has come to be accepted as the standard by many modern Pure Land Buddhists, but it is a radical departure from the origins and faith of a millenium of Pure Land practitioners. Despite its deviance from the ontological commitments of the early Pure Land Buddhists, even this interpretation is not like the materialists' assertions that there is no heaven because the known physical world is all that exists. Rather, it asserts in a truly Buddhist fashion that the Pure Land is not a distant place, but a transcendent reality of which we can become conscious here and now through proper practice.

The widely reported deathbed experiences of Pure Land believers served to confirm the conviction of the validity of this source of knowledge. We will review just a sampling of important cases as representative of the phenomenology of deathbed experiences of Pure Land Buddhists.

Deathbed Experiences in China and Japan

There are occasional pre-Buddhist accounts of Chinese visiting heaven on their deathbeds, or dying and later reviving to describe their experiences to astounded witnesses.[37] Before Amida came to the fore, there were already accounts of visions of heavens opening at the death of Tao-an, a devotee of Maitreya, and others.[38] It is not surprising that the majority of such accounts, however, are found within the Pure Land tradition, which placed such great emphasis on the moment of death and on recording the events surrounding that moment.

Among the disciples of Lu-shan Hui-yuan, one by the name of Seng-chi had a dream while very ill that the Buddha of light took him through the void of the whole universe. He awoke free from all signs of disease and suffering. The next night he sought his sandals, said that he must leave, and then lay down and died, staring into the void with joyful anticipation on his face.[39]

Hui-yuan's star disciple, Hui-yung, in the throes of a grave illness in 414, suddenly asked for his clothes and sandals, folded his hands, and tried to stand, as if he were seeing something. "When the attendant monks asked him what he saw, he replied, 'The Buddha is coming.' When he finished speaking, he died."[40]

The first Pure Land master recognized by most Japanese scholars is T'an-luan, who "saw a golden gate open before him" while recovering from a grave illness. This inspired him to seek more knowledge about the afterlife. He studied first Taoist and then Buddhist texts, finally accepting as the truth the Pure Land sutras (which their translator Bodhiruci probably conveyed to him).[41]

T'an Luan's spiritual disciple, Tao-ch'o, also had a grave illness at age sixty-five. He felt himself to be dying when he suddenly had a vision of T'an-luan, who commanded him to continue teaching.[42] It is recorded that T'an-luan's voice was heard and heavenly flowers were seen by all present. Thereupon

Tao-ch'o quickly recovered, gained a new set of teeth, and was revered like a god by his disciples as he continued to preach for eighteen more years.[43]

It was Chia-ts'ai, who lived shortly after Tao-ch'o, who compiled the first collection of deathbed experiences, the *Ching-t'u-lun*.[44] Of the twenty accounts collected, half are of monks and half are of laypersons. In at least the case of Master Chu-hung, not only the dying person but all present were said to have seen the body of the Buddha coming from the Pure Land in welcome.[45] In other cases, devout laywomen and laymen have visions of heavenly hosts at their deathbeds.[46] In yet another account, a butcher had first a vision of hell that terrified him into chanting the name of Amida, whereupon he had a vision of Amida offering him the lotus seat, and passed away.[47] By the eleventh century such accounts numbered more than one hundred. Whalen Lai typifies deathbed descriptions as follows:

> The "visitation" scene is the climax and this usually involves mysterious fragrance, light, clouds, or colors (the best of the senses) and on rare occasions, actual ascent to the West. . . . Visions of hells or Pure Lands are common, and no doubt Shan-tao's evangelical zeal in depicting these contrasting destinies in picture helped in inculcating an appreciation of the splendors and horrors of the two alternatives.[48]

In Japan, the first distinctly Buddhist compilation of miracles is the *Ryōiki*. Recensions of the *Ryōiki* date from 822 A.D.; its stories date mostly from the period 724–796. Some of these accounts provide specific names, dates (down to the hour and day) and locations for their occurences, a fact favoring their historicity.[49] The *Ryōiki* contains many accounts of human visits to the land of the dead, usually by someone who dies and is revived a few days later. The revived persons tell of their experiences in bright clouds and golden mountains (1.5), in golden palaces (1.30, 2.16), or in a hell where sinners are judged by Yamarāja, god of the dead, from which they are sent back and revived (2.19, 3.9).[50]

In the *Nihon Ōjō Gokurakuki* (ca. 985–6), not only monks but also commoners see the Pure Land or Maitreya's heaven while temporarily dead.[51] In the *Konjaku Monogatari* of the eleventh century, the Bodhisattva Jizō (Sanskrit: *Ksitigarbha*) saves or escorts the dying people because of their morality or their worship of him during their lives.[52] Carmen Blacker summarizes: "A remarkable number of tales can be found which describe a priest who falls sick and dies. For one reason or another his funeral is delayed and . . . he suddenly comes back to life. He has meanwhile been on a long and strange journey, he tells his astonished disciples and friends. . . . They cross a dismal river and eventually arrive at a glittering palace."[53]

Similar tales of deathbed revival with visions of Jizō, Maitreya, or Amida are reported in the *Fusō Ryakki*, compiled in the mid-twelfth century. It covers events through 1094.[54] The *Fusō Ryakki* is important partly for its accounts found in no other sources, and partly because its compiler was the eminent monk Kōen of Enryakuji, who taught and ordained Hōnen.[55]

The *Uji Shūi Monogatari* is variously dated from 1188 to 1215, with the latter date most strongly favored by scholars.[56] It has accounts of revived corpses who report having been saved by Jizō (3.12–13), admonished to lead holier lives (8.4), or even find that Jizō and Yamarāja are one and the same (6.1). An increasing incidence of tales of hell over tales of the Pure Land may reflect the troubles of that uncertain era.

In Kamakura Japan, the *Genkō Shakushō* became yet another prominent source of resuscitation records. In one case, the monk Ennō dies (at age fifty-seven) and revives only to find himself deaf and dumb for three years. When he regains his faculties he speaks of the Pure Land, Maitreya's Palace, Yama's hells, and a miraculous rescue by six figures of Jizō bodhisattva.[57]

The catalogue of Buddhist rebirth tales continues even up to the present century.[58] But these examples should suffice to show that in each century, there have been either documented cases, or at least overwhelming and widespread belief in the possibility of visiting the Pure Land or hell and later returning to the world.

Nor should we assume that the scholars who recorded such tales were all credulous, uncritical, or propagandizers. Pure Land Buddhists found philosophical support in the coherency and consistency of the visions described in several sources: the authority of the sutras; the visions of practicing meditators; and the experiences of real people on their deathbeds, or during temporary death.

Sixteenth century Chu-hung, among others, was particularly concerned with the status of the objects experienced in these states. He concluded that although there was a sense in which they were mind dependent, the fact that everyone at death reports essentially similar imagery demonstrates that the Pure Land is indeed intersubjective and substantial and not hallucinatory or illusory.[59]

So, Pure Land Buddhists would say that the Pure Land is immediately given through phenomenal experience, and also that this experience is confirmed by and found consistent with several types of testimony based on others' experiences. Moreover, the concept of a Pure Land above the realm of samsara fits well with a theory of idealism that makes sense of both this and future worlds in a way that a materialistic metaphysics cannot.

The Move to Mantra Recitation

Throughout the history of Sino-Japanese Pure Land Buddhism, there is considerable discussion of the proper practice, called meditation (Sanskrit: *smrti*; Chinese: *nien*; Japanese: *nen*). It is clear that the hieroglyphic character originally meant "to think on" or "to hold in mind." All three Pure Land sutras stress that, whatever other practices might enable one's birth in the Pure Land, holding in mind the thought of Amida and the Pure Land is a minimal prerequisite. Pictures, sutras, or mantras might be used as aids to visualization, but the central process is one of meditation.[60]

By the time of the Chinese patriarch T'an-luan (ca. 488–554), Chinese Buddhists were already feeling pressure to simplify and concretize Indian meditative practices into forms more familiar and accessible to the Chinese. T'an-luan still preferred to use nien as meditation (or thinking continuously on the Buddha), but sometimes he reluctantly consented to oral recitation of Amida's name in preference to the even less meditative practice of brush writing.[61]

The later patriarchs, however, were even more convinced of the infirmities of their age and of the need of simple practices for ignorant laymen. Therefore, they placed increasing emphasis on a recitative mantra calling on the name of Amitāyus (Chinese: *nien-fo*; Japanese: *nembutsu*).[62] Neither Tao-ch'o nor Shan-tao excluded a range of other practices including discipline and meditation. But in popular practice, the recitative aspect of nien-fo began to usurp the meditative focus from this time.[63]

This change from meditative to recitative emphasis contributed to the increasing popularity of Pure Land Buddhism in the lay community. At the same time, it deprived such practitioners of a tool that had been crucial to the verification of scriptures in their personal meditative experience.

The process of secularization continued in Japan. In the Nara period, Chikō and Gyōki had had impressive visions of the Pure Land,[64] and in the Heian period, Genshin's rebirth tales and paintings had been based on his visions. But it was rather the images themselves, and the song-and-dance nembutsu practiced by wandering monks like Kūya, which led to the spread of Pure Land Buddhism in Japan.[65] In Hōnen, we see the almost paradoxical situation of a master of meditation, with many personal visions of the Pure Land, writing in secret that recitation of the name of Amida is adequate to assure rebirth in the Pure Land at death, while traditional meditating Buddhists denounced such heresies.[66] Hōnen saw the accessibility of the

Pure Land at death as positively encouraging; that even without meditating, common men could achieve the Pure Land at death if they kept their minds fixed on the grace of Amida.

It was Hōnen's disciple Shinran who saw the logical consequences of this move: if people were really powerless to meditate or save themselves in this degenerate age, then even recitation could have no salvific power. Salvation was totally beyond human power and available only through the power of Amida. In this context, the nembutsu became merely a cry of hope or gratitude.[67] Shinran's letters made clear that he expected to live an individual, personal life with his disciples and friends in another world after death.[68] But Shinran abandoned meditation, along with the celibacy and vegetarianism prerequisite to successful visionary meditation. This deprived him of the ability to meditatively confirm his fate while living on earth, and left him vacillating in continual doubt.[69]

Furthermore, Shinran reinterpreted many traditional Buddhist terms to suit his own reformed theology. Rebirth (*ōjō*) he took to mean simply the experience of feeling Amida's grace in this world. *Raigō* he changed from "Amida's welcome at the deathbed" to mean "Amida's bringing us home [in this life]." Nirvana, which used to refer to an unqualifiable state experienceable only in meditation or upon dissolution of the personality, Shinran treated as a blissful but still personal state hoped for after death.[70] Thus, Shinran thoroughly secularized Buddhism, leaving the way open for new interpretations that the Pure Land was simply a state of faith to be gained here and now or a useful psychological myth with no deeper ontological ground.[71]

Modern Japanese Pure Land schools teach nembutsu mantra recitation alone and remain largely agnostic on the crucial philosophical question of personal survival of death in the Pure Land.[72] But if there were really nothing more after death, then this recitation and devotionalism is at best an object-less delusion, and the Pure Land tradition is reduced to a hollow, man-made mythology. It is important, therefore, to distinguish the ontologically noncommittal modern Pure Land sects from the philosophically rich traditions from which they depart.

Traditional Pure Land Buddhists could justify their knowledge of the Pure Land on several mutually supporting grounds. They could point to the phenomenologically self-validating character of direct experience, and to the correspondence between descriptions given in the scriptures and the visions they had while in meditation. To the challenge that daily worldly experiences somehow show their trances to be hallucinatory, they had several replies in favor of their metaphysical idealism: (1) the idea that the commonsense world is more real than the visionary is no more than an unprovable assumption; (2) the idealistic account of visionary experience makes better sense than the materialistic, for materialists are unable to explain in physico-chemical terms either mental events or the similarities of the images of different persons' visions; (3) the idealistic account also makes better sense of survival, which is necessarily of the mind since the corpse does not survive.

If conscious survival of any form at all is accepted, the Buddhists' idealistic world view is more consistent than either the view of an ontological dualism that must somehow explain the relations of matter and mind, or the view of an ontological materialism that cannot deal with the survival of disembodied consciousness.

Implications for Modern Scholarship

The issues addressed in this chapter have significant implications for modern scholarship in the areas of psychology, religion, and philosophy. Let us consider each in turn.

Correspondence with Medical Evidence

It is fascinating to note the many parallels between the descriptions of the Pure Land seen at death or in meditation and the results of contemporary statistical surveys of what people see in Near Death Experiences (NDEs).[73] Compassionate figures of golden light leading the dying person to a realm of peace and joy with multicolored flowers, splendid trees, lakes, and pavilions are reported as frequently by modern Westerners as by ancient Chinese.

The peace and mood elevation promised by the sutras is widely observed among modern patients who have deathbed visions that enable them to forget or transcend their physically painful conditions. Patients resuscitated from death generally report having visited a realm free from all personal conflict in which communication is accomplished through thought alone.

The Buddhists' dark tubular calyx that eventually blossoms into the land of light is a good metaphor for the experiences of many subjects who report being drawn through a dark tube or tunnel. Sensations of a tube, of floating, of hearing a rush of wind, of time and space distortion, may all be caused by malfunctions of the temporal lobe in drugged or near-death situations.[74] Magnification or enlargement of images and shining geometric patterns or jeweled "Indra's nets" are common to both the later sutras and to many hallucinatory drug trips.[75]

This is not to reduce such experiences to purely physiological interpretations that are clearly inadequate to account for the range of phenomena, and which may be correlates but not causes of the experiences in any case.[76] Rather, the more important point is the relative universality of such experiences in disparate cultures and ages, and their dramatic impact on the lives of those who encounter them.

It is impossible to judge at this point whether these visions are archetypes dredged up from some collective unconscious at the moment of death, projections of subliminal wish-fulfillments common to all humans, or genuine glimpses into another realm which follows this one. None of the above hypotheses has any a priori preferability over rival claimants.

We cannot but be struck by the similarity both of the experiences reported and of the arguments used to interpret them (e.g., by Chu-hung in medieval China and by the Society for Psychical Research in modern New York). The extreme coincidence of modern data with accounts from medieval China and Japan tends to reinforce the conclusion that such experiences really happened and were not simply trumped-up hoaxes or cultural myths alone. Even accounts of deathbed visions and of white or purple clouds in the death chamber need not be written off as hagiography, since we have similar reports by Western witnesses in this century.[77] It is worth bearing in mind that such experiences are neither new nor unique to any single culture.

Source of Amida Imagery

The above discussion also leads us to a stronger position on the origins of Pure Land thought. Western critics of Pure Land Buddhism have suggested that it was a Chinese adaptation and distortion of Indian Christianity (Dahlmann), or a borrowing of Zoroastrianism or Manichaeism via the silk routes.[78] However, as we have noted, the idea of salvation by faith alone came to flourish in Japan only after the twelfth century, devoid of Christian influence. Moreover, we must acknowledge a meditative basis for the descriptions of the Sanskrit and Chinese Pure Land sutras. It was the meditative experience of the Chinese themselves that enabled visionaries like T'an-luan to accept the newly imported and otherwise very foreign religious texts of Indian Buddhism. The later Chinese commentaries are also based on personal religious experiences in meditation and attending deathbeds, not on a misunderstanding of Christian sources. If parallels are found between the Pure Land theology and that of Christianity, they indicate not borrowing, but the strikingly similar life-changing religious experience of saints and sages in two very different cultures and philosophies.

The similarities of early Christian and early Pure Land religious experience need no more be explained on the basis of contact than do the similarities of either one to modern deathbed experiences prove contact between them. In short, the reason Pure Land Buddhism resembles Christianity is not historical contact, but the similarity of religious experience in both cases.

A Model of an Idealist Next World

In both the scriptural and experiential accounts of the Pure Land, we have a significant description of what the next world might be like. This in itself is enough to rule out the objections of those logical positivists who assert that we cannot even formulate a coherent conception of what an afterlife might be like. But there is a more startling coincidence.

Buddhists have described the Pure Land as a mind-dependent world. It shares certain intersubjective features for all of its inhabitants, has various areas for various types of consciousnesses, and responds in its minor events to the thoughts and wills of its inhabitants or experiencer/creators. This is precisely the same sort of world which philosopher H. H. Price envisioned and defended in making a case for a coherent conception of the afterlife.[79]

There is the same notion that bodies will not really exist in the way they seem to exist in this material world. Still, they will feel equally real and present to those who do not yet realize that both body and discrimination are their own projections. There is the same notion that there will be several different levels of delusion and projection, intersubjective in more or fewer ways, but all of them feeling equally real to their projectors. There is the same notion that there will be no punishment per se, but that gratification of one's physical desires will soon become flat and valueless, while real joy will come in seeking spiritual insight into one's own nature and the nature of Truth (dharma).

In fact, since the Buddhist formulation is even more detailed than Price's, it can help us escape from Price's philosophical difficulties. Price's next world has been criticized because its will-dependent nature leads either to solipsism or incoherence of identity (as when several people desire to speak to the same person in different places at the same time). Price has not made a clear reply.

Pure Land Buddhists explain that objects are projectible and perceptible by the mere thought of or wish for them, but human consciousnesses are still uniquely localized in individually distinct places. So, we may conjure up and phenomenally experience a meal or a bath in the Pure Land by merely thinking of it. But if we wish to speak to other persons, we must seek them wherever they are at that moment (both spatially and psychologically), and await the others' disengagement from their present mental activity so that they may relate to us. So in Pure Land Buddhism, the subjectivity of impressions of objects is not incompatible with a higher objectivity of individual consciousness and the bodies they project.

So far, we have traced Pure Land Buddhism from its origins in early Mahayanism and studied the ontology and epistemology that is presupposed by Pure Land scriptures and practitioners. We have seen parallels between meditations and deathbed experiences, and have seen that idealist ontology makes good sense of both. This indicates, too, that Pure Land Buddhism is not a borrowing from other religions, but a reflection of common religious experience, pointing to a reality envisioned in the West as well: an idealist life after death.

5

Tibetan Buddhism and the *Book of the Dead*

The Tibetan Worldview

TIBET'S UNIQUE GEOGRAPHICAL SETTING has strongly influenced its philosophy and history. Occupying over a million square kilometers in the middle of the Asian continent, Tibet is severely isolated from its neighbors by the Himalaya and Kunlun mountain ranges. Although its snows feed the Mekong, Brahmaputra, Indus, Yangtze, and other rivers, the mountains block out the monsoons from the south, and annual rainfall is extremely scanty. Therefore, the Tibetans can raise few crops and must depend largely on nomadic sheep and yak herding for their livelihoods.

Tibet's barren plateaus range from eleven thousand to eighteen thousand feet in altitude, where oxygen becomes too thin for the unacclimated visitor. Because of the extreme altitude the daily sun is very strong, but at night temperatures plunge to freezing even in the summertime. The winter adds to the subzero temperatures the perils of blizzards, hailstorms, and windstorms carrying abrasive gravel and destructive stones. Thus, the land has never been particularly hospitable, and this environment early gave rise to its inhabitants' beliefs in malevolent superhuman powers. More than in other countries, the unusual environmental conditions of Tibet were a strong influence on the philosophy and worldviews of its people.[1]

Pre-Buddhist Tibetan Philosophy and Religion

The meat-eating habits of the nomadic Tibetans stand in obvious opposition to the Buddhist philosophy and lifestyle in semitropical India. Since boiling temperatures are lower at high altitudes, and boiled dishes provide a warming relief from the cold, boiling is the chief means of cooking, further robbing the Tibetans' already limited diet of needed nutrients. Taken together, a poor diet, severe climate, lack of oxygen, and frequent bouts with plagues early disposed Tibetans to take for granted many hallucinatory and paranormal experiences. This in turn led to their ready acceptance of philosophies that explained such phenomena and placed them in a systematized picture of the universe. The first of these systematized philosophies was known as the *Bon.*

Like the early Chinese philosophies, the Bon religion held that there were twin spirits in humans (*pho-lha* and *dGralha*) that cooperate to protect and govern them and that depart at death for other realms.[2] Shortly after death, if not properly exorcised, the disembodied spirits of humans were said to haunt their former habitations or sites of death.[3] Malevolent spirits inhabiting the air, earth, and water were held to cause sickness and death unless propitiated by human or animal sacrifices (these were replaced by effigies after the advent of Buddhism).

After death, the souls of virtuous people were thought to ascend to heaven, while wicked souls were condemned by the lord of demons, *rTsiu* (*Yamarāja*), to vividly described hells.[4] To assist the soul in its postmortem adventures, the corpse was carefully interred with clothes and provisions—a striking contrast to the later Buddhist practices of cremation or dismemberment and exposure. The Bon beliefs that shamans could communicate with the spirits of the dead through trance possession, or could visit the world of the dead and return, persisted to influence the Tibetan interpretation of Tantric Buddhism when it arrived.[5]

It would be unfair to dismiss Bon as mere animism; several Bon ideas play decisive roles in Tibetan Buddhism's development. Concern with control of nature is undeniably present in both. More importantly, Bon had already accorded a central role to death and funeral ceremonies, and Tibetan Buddhism was to continue this theme in a way quite foreign to Indian Buddhism.

The non-Buddhist notions that there is an intermediate period during which the soul may return, that there is a judgment followed by heavens and hells, and that living persons can communicate with the dead, all find their places in Tibetan Buddhism. Tucci claims that the original ideas of hell came from India but that the Tibetans supplemented the Indians' visions of "hot hells" with their own "cold hells," founded on their own deathbed experiences: "The Tibetan, with his tendency to the macabre, drew an even grimmer picture of hot and cold hells and frightful tortures which are dwelt on in a hair-raising literature, the *delo*. This is a series of accounts given by those who, on the brink of death, caught a glimpse of life beyond the tomb, but then returned to tell of the terrifying things they saw."[6]

Whether Tibetan ideas of hell came originally from Bon or

from India may be impossible to prove conclusively, but we do know they were an important theme in Tibetan thought by the time Buddhism arrived. Within the early Tibetan folk tradition there are also many accounts of those who died, passed on to judgment and hell, and returned to life to describe their experiences a few days later.[7] Again, there are descriptions of yogic masters who went to the Tusita heavens to commune with their dead masters while in a trance[8] and then returned to normal waking life in this world, following the example of Asanga, the founder of the Yogācāra Buddhist school.[9]

There was widespread agreement between Bon and popular Buddhism that prayer services and ceremonies could vicariously assist the progress of the departed souls, somewhat parallel to the *Ullambana* (Japanese: *O-bon*) services in China and Japan.[10] Such facts also refute the Christian prejudice that similarities in liturgy and doctrine concerning the afterlife must be borrowings from the Christian tradition, which after all did not reach the borders of Tibet until the fifteenth century.[11]

The important point here is that the Tibetans, like the Chinese before them, did not adopt Buddhism in its entirety merely out of political or aesthetic considerations. They accepted Buddhism insofar as it clarified processes that they already knew and as it illustrated new truths that they had not yet verbalized. An oversimplified approach might suggest that Buddhism brought to these countries certain views of heaven, hell, and the afterlife. The evidence cited here documents that such views actually predated Buddhism in each separate location, and indeed that the real deathbed experiences of people in each of these cultures modified Buddhism itself.

Vajrayāna Buddhism

In previous chapters, we observed the evolution of Buddhism from a strict disciplinary system in which each individual might achieve cessation of rebirth (nirvana) by his own detachment from desires (Hīnayāna Buddhism) to a pietistic religion in which the power and grace of Amida was taken to be the ultimate determinant of salvation in a gilded heaven (Mahayana Buddhism). The third of the Buddhist *yānas*, or vehicles, and the last in its philosophical and chronological development, was the *Vajrayāna* or *Tantrayāna*.

Vajra means diamond and symbolizes the indestructible, absolute, or void. *Tantra* means "thread" or "cord" and refers to the uninterrupted chain of teachers who supposedly passed these teachings down from generation to generation. In short, the Vajrayāna or Tantrayāna is concerned with ultimately achieving the absolute and is passed on orally from master to disciple. It is an esoteric philosophy bordering on mystery religion. To attain this self-identification with and understanding of the absolute, it advocates mantras (spells), mudras (hand gestures), and visual meditation on mandalas.[12]

As Vajrayāna Buddhism depends on a lineage of teachers and disciples, it has directed more attention to the personalities of its various teachers than to their doctrinal disagreements. Buddhism was first formally introduced in the years 747–749 A.D. by Rinpoche (Padma Sambhava) from the Indian university of Nalanda. Despite its rapid assimilation of Bon ideas, Buddhism faced repeated opposition from both the government and Bon priesthood. In the eleventh century, Atisa, Marpa, and others arrived from India to create vigorous new Tibetan sects of Buddhism. Meanwhile, the previous Bon Buddhists "discovered" hidden sutras in order to give themselves fresh claims to authority.

Cosmology and the *Trikāya* Doctrine

Mythologically, Vajrayāna Buddhism developed a system of five Great Buddhas, lords of the four directions and the center, namely, Vairocana, Aksobhya, Ratnasambhava, Amoghasiddhi, and Amitābha. These are all taken to be visible manifestations of the ineffable and primordial *Ādi-buddha*, the void or absolute. It is thought that other buddhas and bodhisattvas, such as Avalokitesvara (Kwan-yin), Bhaisajya-guru, Maitreya, and their female counterparts, also exist on this level.[13]

The *trikāya* (three-body) doctrine is essential to Vajrayāna philosophy. We have seen that in Pure Land Buddhism, there was already the idea that Amida and other bodhisattvas have three bodies: an earthly body (aeons in the past), a superphysical body (now in heaven), and a law body (one with truth or dharma). In Vajrayāna Buddhism, the three *kāyas*, or bodies, point to different levels of reality.[14]

Ultimately, the only real is Mind, the Absolute, formless Truth and Light, which is the body of Law, or *dharmakāya*. As in Mahayana Buddhism, the buddhas and bodhisattvas possess bodies of spirit and light that seem to have form but are essentially the projections of the dharmakāya. This spiritual form of spiritual beings just short of total selfless nirvana is called the *sambhogakāya*.

Finally, there is the material level of the *nirmānakāya*, the body in which humans and animals, mountains, and dreams are perceived. This realm, although analogous to the modern realists' world, differs from it in two important respects. First, it includes levels of subtle matter, invisible to our eyes but equally real, in which exist demons, ghosts, titans, and gods. These, along with humans and animals, comprise the six worlds. These apparently divine beings are unlike the bodhisattvas' sambhogakāyas in that they are still composed of subtle substances and are thus still subject to laws of causation and rebirth.

Then the Vajrayāna goes one step further: it asserts that *all* phenomena and experiences are ultimately no more than the illusory projections of consciousness—the material level being merely a grosser distortion of truth and reality than the spiritual level.

Mind-Only Doctrine

In the fourth century A.D., the philosophers Asanga and Vasubandhu formalized the Yogācāra (mind-only) Sect of Buddhism. As its name implies, this system of absolute idealism held that nothing is real outside of the mind. There exist both individual minds and the ultimate absolute mind of which they are emanations. The logical demonstration of these conclusions is predicated on the Buddhist principle that all phenomena are fleetingly perceived but impermanent and therefore ultimately unreal. The empirical basis of these conclusions, however, was the ancient tradition of Indian yoga.

In yoga, lengthy meditations lead first to the paranormal powers such as those the Buddha attained and ultimately to the realization of the illusoriness of all material appearances. In the Yogācāra view, there is a sense in which any experience is just as real as any other, whether apparently internal and hallucinatory or ostensibly external and objective. All that is ultimately real and continuous of the individual is the pure subject, the mind store (*ālaya-vijñāna*), although it, too, changes. It is this mind store, or ālaya-vijñāna, that experiences, judges, contemplates, and remembers, thus constituting a locus of identity and continuity through many apparent bodies, or lifetimes.

It might well be argued that the ālaya-vijñāna concept is merely a rehabilitation of the old Hindu notion of ātman, without the insistence on its ontological permanence and immutability. The early Buddhist perspective says that phenomena are all that exist and that the apparent self is determined by the phenomena that it encounters. The Yogācāra philosophy, by contrast, says that mind is all that exists, and all apparent phenomena are merely its own projections.

Coupled with the belief in mystic teachings, the concept that all is only mind has tremendous implications for Vajrayāna Buddhism. If all is only mind, the process of death and rebirth is no longer an inevitable aspect of an external reality to which all must submit. It then becomes unnecessary to physically undergo a long succession of lifetimes, for by changing one's conscious thoughts, the whole sequence can be broken or abridged. Even the law of karma is elevated to an entirely different level. No longer are physical actions seen as having inevitable physical effects. Rather, mental acts are the only acts that have any effects at all, either in apparently external happenings or in apparently internal feelings and visions. Karmic determination of an individual's future good or ill can thus also be avoided or aborted by mental purification and concentration.

Mantras, mudras, and samadhi are required to affect this change of consciousness necessary to attain nirvana. Here, too, the Vajrayāna departs from orthodox Samkhya Yoga, in allowing the consumption of meat and wine, and even intercourse with women, encouraging at each step the realization that none of these phenomena are ultimately real. Under the tutelage of a Vajrayāna Lama (guru), the student expects to develop psychic powers, to leave his body, and to experience the Absolute in trance. Thus, he will prepare himself for the moment of death when he will direct his consciousness out of his body and into final union with Truth (dharmakaya), rather than allowing any further cycles of rebirth.[15]

We have here treated the Vajrayāna school as a significant departure from the ontology and practice of Gautama Siddhartha. Many Vajrayāna Buddhists believe that the historic Buddha shared their views but concealed those teachings because his immediate followers were not ready for them. Most scholars, however, believe either that the Buddha held no opinion on ontology whatsoever or that he was a phenomenal realist, accepting the existence of things outside of the mind, and in fact believing that the mind could not subsist by itself. This debate need not be resolved here, if it is clear at least how the Vajrayāna differs from these views.

The Book of the Dead

The vastness of Tibet, the repeated introductions of Buddhism by different Indian monks in different regions, and the varying degrees of assimilation of the old Bon religion into the new Vajrayāna Buddhism all account for the development of numerous schools of Buddhism within Tibet. There are several excellent histories of Tibetan Buddhism that thoroughly discuss the details of these sects.[16] More important is the fact that ultimately all the sects came to use the *Book of the Dead* as their central scripture for matters concerning death, dying, and the states immediately following death. More than any other Buddhist text, this book purports to explain the experiences of consciousness after the death of the body, and it is therefore of particular interest and relevance to this present study.

While early Buddhism tended to deny the possibility of disembodied consciousness between death and rebirth, the Buddhist tradition soon developed the idea of just such an intermediate state after death, called *antarābhava*.[17] This state was little discussed, but it accounted for the personal and psychic continuity needed between a person's death and the rebirth of that consciousness in another body. Mahayana Buddhism had already rehabilitated the soul, alias the ālaya-vijñāna, which was thought to continue from one body to another. So it was natural that Vajrayānists should also welcome the concept of an intermediate state between incarnations, called the *bardo* in Tibetan.

The sutra called the *Bardo Thodol* (or *thosgroll*) is for "Salvation by Hearing While in the Intermediate State."[18] It is read to the soul of the dying or dead person, to explain to the soul the various phenomena that it will encounter and to encourage it toward a desirable rebirth. The text of the Bardo Thodol, or *Book of the Dead*, as it is commonly translated, purports to date back to the founder of Tibetan Buddhism, Padma Sambhava himself. There is no doubt that many of the teachings therein are indeed of great age, for both the imagery and philosophy show traces of Bon influence. However, the first known uses of the *Book of the Dead* date to the eleventh century, when it was miraculously discovered among the many treasure writings (*gTermas*) which Padma Sambhava was said to have buried for posterity.[19]

Some of these writings are obviously fakes designed to lend an aura of authenticity to the old Nying-ma-pa Buddhist school in the face of Buddhist reform and innovation in the eleventh century. Its doubtful authorship notwithstanding, similar versions of the *Book of the Dead* gained wide acceptance among all the major Tibetan Buddhist sects. This demonstrates its inherent compatibility with the Tibetan worldview. Lama Govinda's statement is representative of the general view of Tibetans:

> The descriptions of those visions which, according to the *Bardo Thodol*, appear in the intermediate state (bardo) following death are neither primitive folklore nor theological speculations. They are not concerned with the appearances of supernatural beings, like gods, spirits, or genii, but with the visible projections or reflexes of inner processes, experiences, and states of mind, produced in the creative phase of meditation. . . . The *Bardo Thodol* is first of all a book for the living, to prepare them not only for the dangers of death, but to give them an opportunity to make use of the great possibilities which offer themselves in the moment of relinquishing the body.[20]

This sacred text was thought to have been verified by the meditations of yogins in this lifetime, and it invited others to test its truth by similar practices of meditation. It served simultaneously as a description of what dying men and yogins in death-like trances have experienced, and also as a guide on how to deal with such experiences in one's own meditations and finally in death.

Traditional Deathbed Practices

The mind or soul (Tibetan: *sems*) of the dead person is thought to linger around its corpse for several days after the cessation of breathing. While unable to speak, it can see and hear all that goes on. The *Book of the Dead* is read in the home in the presence of the corpse (and soul) to protect and encourage it. It is said that even when the soul goes through terrifying or surrealistic visual experiences, it can still hear the *Book of the Dead* being read, echoing like a soundtrack behind the other worldly visual imagery it experiences.

In fact, religious practice at death is neither so simple nor unified. It is not unusual to find several services conducted at once: a Bon service chasing evil spirits out of the house and convincing the spirit of the dead man that he is indeed dead and must leave; a Pure Land service invoking Amida to come to the deathbed and escort the soul of the believer to heaven; and a bardo service occupying one or several weeks, in which the *Book of the Dead* is read to guard and guide the soul through its immediate postmortem adventures.[21]

Some may doubt the depth of belief or criticize the timing of these apparently incongruous practices, but they are not as contradictory as they may seem at first sight. There is a sense in which the bardo allows each soul its own choice from among these options: to become a ghost, to be reborn in the Pure Land, or to transcend everything. One authority suggests that these variations depend upon the spiritual advancement of the deceased: the average man will experience a loss of consciousness before awakening in the bardo state, the especially pious man will see gods and gurus come to greet him at his deathbed, and trained yogins will pass directly into higher states with no loss of consciousness.[22]

Tibetan Buddhism recognizes from the outset that death is not an instantaneous occurrence, such as when the breath stops or the heart no longer beats. Rather, death is seen as a long process taking hours or even days, during which a variety of sensations and experiences accompany each successive stage of the dissolution of the human personality from its bodily habitation. In particular, the eight stages of death are accompanied respectively by the following experiences:

1. Shrinking of the limbs, the impression of sinking, and seeing a cloud or mirage.
2. Cessation of hearing, drying of the mouth, and an appearance of blue billowing smoke.
3. Cessation of smell, cooling of the body, and an appearance of lights "like fireflies."
4. Cessation of taste, end of breath and movement, and vision as of a sputtering butter lamp.
5. Cessation of all conceptions, and vision of vacuous empty whiteness like moonlight.
6. Energy moving from the sexual organ to the heart, and a red-orange appearance arising.
7. Heart energy lost, cessation of dualism, and vision of radiant black vacuity like autumn night.
8. Blood or phlegm leaving the nose or sexual organ and an appearance of clear light.[23]

Now it is not completely explicit whether this is a descriptive or prescriptive account, in other words, whether this is taken to be a true description of what everyone necessarily experiences during the death process, or whether we are to understand that most people should pass through some such stages. There seems room for broad interpretation and exception in the commentary, and of course the account presupposes people who are dying natural deaths, not in accidents, seizures, or sudden explosions. The interesting point of this account, however, is that it yields a chronology of death that is potentially capable of empirical verification or falsification.

Commentators consider the above chronology to be simply the physiological effects of the disintegration or dissociation of the consciousness from the body, a physical but not spiritually important phenomenon. More important is the location from which the soul or semimaterial consciousness leaves the corpse. There are said to be several places from which the soul may leave the body, but it will fall into subhuman wombs unless it leaves by the parietal aperture (at the top of the head where the skull is joined). This is the rationale given for not touching the corpse except by the priests and their helpers, who try to coax the soul out from the top of the head by pulling out some hairs.[24]

The departure of the soul at death is thought to be identical to that departure of the soul discussed in the literature of out-of-body experiences or astral projection, feats commonly attributed to accomplished yogins.[25] When the consciousness is transferred out of the body, in a process called *pho-wa* in Tibetan, it is thought to be able to travel freely over distances, or to take up the (dead) body of some other creature. Meditative pho-wa, or soul travel, is considered highly dangerous; it is only to be undertaken by the adept under the careful guidance of a guru, while someone else remains to protect the original body.[26]

The important point is that in both yoga and Buddhism, the processes involved in meditative travel and death are essentially alike. The only major difference between the yogic trance and death is that in trance the soul returns to its body after its sojourns, while at death it cannot do so. Tibetans also noted the striking similarity of experiences of those in trances and those revived from death or near death. Now let us turn our attention to the *Book of the Dead* as a chronology of the phenomenology of conscious experience after death.

The Three Stages of the *Bardo*

According to the *Book of the Dead,* there are three stages in the bardo, or intermediate disembodied state following death. Each of these stages corresponds to an opportunity to enter a different level of existence in an ontologically different form, namely the dharmakaya, sambhogakāya, and nirmanakāya.[27]

The first stage is called the *Chikhai Bardo.* There,

... at the moment of death, the empiric consciousness, or consciousness of objects, is lost. This is what is popularly called a "swoon," which is however the corollary of superconsciousness itself, or of the Clear Light of the Void. . . . This empiric consciousness disappears, unveiling Pure Consciousness, which is ever ready to be "discovered" by those who have the will to seek and the power to find it. That clear, colourless Light is a sense-symbol of the formless Void . . . the negation of all determinations, but not of "Is-ness" as such . . . it is the Perfect Experience which is Buddhahood . . . consciousness freed of all limitation . . . *Nirvāna.*"[28]

This vision of pure light may be accompanied by "such a Dazzlement as is produced by an infinitely vibrant landscape in the Springtide."[29] It may also remind one of transparent moonlight sometimes mistaken for heaven, but most often analogized to a blindingly clear, open sky.[30] The dying consciousness is advised to identify itself with this light and abandon all traces of self-identification or self-consciousness. Some observers take the halo around a dying saint to be evidence of such identification with the absolute Truth and Light.

For the enlightened saint or yogin, this is the consummation of existence: personal consciousness is transcended, temporality is no more, and there is only the unqualifiable "suchness" of nirvana. Lesser yogins or blessed people may be able to retain this vision of the light for several days, but they are eventually pulled away from it by their other desires or deluded habits of thinking. For still others, the experience may be no more than a brief flash of light.[31] Bound by their karmic cravings and habits of believing in illusions, they regress downwards to other levels.

In the second stage, called the *Chonyid Bardo*, the consciousness clothes itself with a psychically projected body which mirrors the physical body that it had once projected on this material plane. Over the course of seven days, the seven benign Buddhas appear to the consciousness: the pentad of Vairocana, Aksobhya, Ratnasambhava, Amoghasiddhi, and Amitābha described above, then the Buddha representing the combined deities of the six realms, and then the Buddha representing the "wisdom-holding deities." Each of these Buddhas is symbolized as a blinding colored light with imagery like that of the Tibetan *tanka* paintings.

Again, the soul is urged to identify itself with these lights, for it still has these seven chances to bring itself into spiritual one-ness with these Buddhas. If successful, it may dwell indefinitely on their higher planes as a bodhisattva, with no need for further rebirth and with ideal conditions for progress towards final nirvana. On the other hand, if at any point it is repelled by these visions because of its recognition of its own impurities—or if it is more attracted to the dull lights of the lower sensual realms in the opposite direction—it will be reborn into one of the six realms of worldly existence. There is some disagreement among the various sects as to the exact color and order of appearance of the seven Buddhas, but this question is of little importance to our study.[32]

Through these seven days of Buddha manifestations, if the dead person's consciousness has neither identified with any of the luminosities nor has fled to any lower realm, it then con-fronts another seven periods in which terrifying deities appear. The *Book of the Dead* encourages the soul to see these gruesome apparitions also as mere projections of its own subconscious, to embrace and absorb them without fear, rather than accepting their reality and fleeing from them.

Catholic interpreter Tucci explains:

> The forces thus represented are present in all of us and go to make up our personality of which they form the underlying pattern; they are therefore also the means of salvation, when our *gnosis*, on understanding their nature, absorbs them. This is the knowledge that annihilates, bringing us back from the apparent to the real, a return to our origin. . . . When recognition is absent, such visions would be regarded as the god of death,

and death would be believed to be a reality, and the dead man caught up in the succeeding phases of the karmic process."[33]

These terrifying apparitions must not be thought of as the evil counterparts of the previous "good" Buddhas, for in Vajrayāna Buddhism there is neither good nor evil. In fact, both the Buddhas and these *Herukas*, or lords of death, are no more than the projections of the subconscious mind. One can attain spiritual rebirth by knowing that all is spirit, by identifying with these brilliant or terrifying images and granting neither them nor oneself any objective reality. If the consciousness has still been unable to yogically identify with any of these apparitions during the first two weeks after death, then it proceeds still further into a period of prematerial existence.

The third period, called the *Sidpa Bardo*, depicts the consciousness clad in a body of subtle matter. Conscious of the material world and its six realms, the soul has the powers of astral projection such as moving instantaneously across distances and through objects. The consciousness first perceives its old home and family in mourning and tries to convince them that it has not died, but to no avail.[34] Unable to reenter its cremated or dismembered corpse, blown by the winds of karma, it wanders forth feeling homeless and miserably alone, realizing for the first time that it is dead to other humans. It may try to rest in graveyards or temples, but as its nature is pure consciousness, which it has not yet learned how to calm and control, it may not rest for long in any one spot. Visions of fearful precipices and chasms and feelings of being crushed or squeezed into crevices are predicted.

Finally, the soul perceives the lord of death and his demons come to judge it.[35] It sees its good and evil deeds weighed, and feels itself racked and hacked by demons. Since its body is a mental projection, it is not destroyed, but continues to feel the (self-)punishments as long as it adheres to and projects the reality of that body and its sins. At last it is released, only to be pursued by furies across many strange landscapes prior to material rebirth.

Transcendence or Rebirth

At any point in this last process of the Sidpa Bardo—as a disembodied soul, as a judged and tortured being, or as a spirit pursued by furies—one may yet escape. One may transcend the whole illusion of misery and suffering by holding in mind Amida, Kannon, or any other patron bodhisattva. If the mind can fix on this imagery, and is able to cast out all other self-created fearful visions, the dead soul may yet rise to the Pure Land or Tusita heavens to avoid further rebirth and meditate in the company of the saints. However, it is much harder to hold an image of Amida in mind while one imagines oneself being tortured than in the earlier period when that image presents itself vividly and naturally in the Chonyid Bardo visualizations. Therefore, not many are able to transcend at this stage, although the *Book of the Dead* is read as a spur in that direction.

The more average consciousness undergoes a seemingly endless period of tortures that actually take place in a few weeks of human time. Chastised in spirit, it again finds itself looking at the six material realms. Premonitory signs of different landscapes indicate the type of body into which the consciousness will be reborn. Seeing beautiful bodies engaged in the sex act, it is drawn towards its old pastime and finds itself inside a womb of its own choosing.

Some interpreters say that the consciousness may be drawn into animal or divine wombs depending on its flight from the furies; others say that all rebirth at this point is on the human level.[36] The *Book of the Dead* urges the consciousness (if it is still listening at all!) not to choose by physical attraction, but to choose a home with parents of pious character and adequate wealth, to permit their offspring to follow the yogic religious path and progress yet higher in his [*sic*] next round of existence.[37]

At their deaths, the saints and great yogins go directly to nirvana or become bodhisattvas in the higher heavens. The great incarnation lamas—spiritual and secular heads of the great monasteries and districts of Tibet—are said to have a somewhat different mode of progression. The *Dalai* (political head) and *Panchen* (spiritual head) lamas are thought to be the material manifestations of the bodhisattvas Kannon and Amida, respectively. Naturally, they undergo no illusions whatsoever during the forty-nine day period during which average souls are said to wander through the three bardos.

Before their deaths, the great lamas indicate the region of the country and the characteristics of the family into which they plan to be reborn. When they die, those regions and families are sought out. Forty-nine days after the lama's passing, babies showing miraculous signs are inspected for birthmarks and other similarities to the departed lama.[38] They are then placed in a room with a number of sacred objects, some of which had belonged to the previous Dalai or Panchen Lama.[39] The baby who shows the most marked preference for those objects alone is then singled out for special attention.

The priests put the chosen child to further tests of identity while conducting divination and prayer ceremonies, and the country is temporarily ruled by a regent. The body of the departed predecessor is carefully preserved in a stūpa (*chorten*). At the age of four, the chosen child assumes the garb and tonsure of a monk, at eight he is made abbot of his convent, and at eighteen he is installed with the full powers of the highest lama.[40]

Thus, there is a sense in which the highest lamas are never discarnate from the world for more than forty-nine days. This is only possible because the bodhisattvas Amida and Kannon are miraculously able to maintain simultaneously both a nirmā-nakāya (fleshly body) in this world and a sambhogakāya (spiritual body) in their respective heavens or Buddha fields. Although the practice of reincarnation lamas dates back only about 500 years, it is accompanied by such miraculous occurrences that even critical Western observers have been impressed.[41] There are elaborate ceremonies surrounding the deaths of incarnate lamas, but there is no need for other monks to read to them from the *Book of the Dead* since they already know the idealistic landscapes to come and how to deal with them.[42]

The *Book of the Dead*, then, is not a Dantean description of eternal heavens and hells. Rather, it is a chronological review of the gateways to numerous postmortem levels of experience during the intermediate state between incarnations, usually lasting twenty-eight to forty-nine days. Its imagery incorporates all of the afterlife possibilities that Buddhists have yet envisioned: nirvanic transcendence, ascension to Pure Lands, judgment and torture, disembodied existence as an invisible ghost, and rebirth in this or other worlds. Its reconciliation of so many traditions is based not on crude eclecticism, but on a profound philosophy of absolute idealism buttressed by a long tradition of experience in yoga meditation.[43]

Philosophical Issues

The thrust of Vajrayāna philosophy is that all of these postmortem and meditative visions are imaginary mental imagery. We may recall Price's discussions of postmortem image worlds and the inabilities of dead people to believe that they had died (paralleled by the experiences predicted in the *Book of the Dead*.)[44] This does not mean, however, that imaginary experiences are any less real than this present world, for its experiences are equally illusory![45] Rather, it suggests two important conclusions.

First, we should try to transcend this illusion of the material world at every opportunity—both through meditation and at death—rather than becoming caught up in its desires and pain.

Second, the structure of even this material world is spiritual and psychological rather than external and physical. Thus, any attempts to explain the ultimate nature of reality according to the physical senses that we presently use or according to the appearances of this material realm are ultimately doomed to failure.

Although there is a measure of shared illusion (intersubjectivity) on each level, the laws and structures of any given realm may be violated at will by one who has yogically perfected his mind and has come to know his own unreality. The Tibetans can also explain their *siddhas*, or miracle-working lamas and yogins, on this model. This idealistic philosophy naturally leads serious students of the Tibetan *Book of the Dead* to predict that the heavens, judgments, and ghostly scenarios described by other religious traditions have equal claims to validity; the afterlife is culturally relative insofar as its imagery is projected by the perceiver, and the perceiver has been conditioned by the culture in which he was educated.[46]

This leaves us with some important philosophical questions. If absolute idealism is indeed correct, do postmortem experiences of consciousness reflect no more than one's preconceptions and expectations? Does this description apply equally to the division of the ideal realm into the three states of transcendence, spirit, and apparent materiality? Are these realms an objective ground of a true idealistic landscape within which all cultures may shape their own illusions? Or are these concepts also subject to the mind of the experiencers?

We can put the question even more bluntly: Is nirvana a real transcendent state to which some non-Buddhists are blind because they do not understand and accept it? Or is even nirvana itself a fiction or illusion that simply seems equally real for the Buddhists whose culture reinforces this concept? Is intersubjectivity of postmortem experience based on cultural similarity, on Jungian archetypes, on the similar physiology of everyone's brains, or on the structure of the idealists' universe?

6

Models for
Survival

WE HAVE SEEN that Buddhists believe in rebirth, that rebirth is not always physical or instantaneous, and that some invisible carrier of consciousness or continuity is required to make sense of rebirth. We have also observed a wide range of possible rebirths within the Buddhist cosmology. We have seen that descriptions of idealist postmortem worlds like the Pure Land are plentiful in Buddhist philosophy, and that Buddhism also contends for the existence of a supra-personal, unconceptualizable state of nirvana.

We have discussed the arguments of Buddhist philosophers through many centuries in very different traditions, and noted the similarities between some of their conclusions. We have seen the meditative and deathbed evidences that might indicate that some aspect of human consciousness survives bodily death. This all leads us to the point where we may ask, "Does consciousness survive bodily death?" If so, what can we conclude about its experiences at death and thereafter? How would the adoption of a survivalist position force us to modify our views of the world? And what sorts of studies might further clarify the nature and status of the afterlife? These are some of the questions that this chapter attempts to answer.

This range of possible Near Death Experiences (NDEs) has already been studied by scholars like Moody and Ring, who itemize a number of stages through which dying people may pass.[1] These are not sequential steps through which everyone will pass, but each of these stages has been reported by someone, so it is quite possible that others will experience them again in the future.

At death, many people experience a whooshing sound, or find themselves passing through a black vortex, tunnel, or void. Some see colorful nets, lights, and geometric imagery. Some have veridical Out-of-Body Experiences (OBEs), and see their bodies from an external vantage point; others have dreamlike hallucinations of chemical origins and doubtful referentiality. Some have visions of departed loved ones, holy figures, or heavenly scenery. Some of these events are at least partly neurophysiological, others are virtually inexplicable except through the survival hypothesis.

We must not forget that most people die, whether in peace or pain, without reporting any remarkable experiences or saving grace.[2] Based on the number of reports alone, it seems that only a minority of dying people have OBEs or NDEs. The number reporting memories of past lives veridically is still far smaller. We are not entitled to jump to the conclusion that everyone will survive death or be reborn. It seems rather more probable that there is a wide range in the ways that different people will experience survival—if indeed they experience anything at all.[3]

An Afterlife Conforming to Personal Expectations

Many books on survival propose that the expectations of the dying persons determine whether and in what way their conscious experiences continue. This is the theory which British philosophers Price and Hick have advocated;[4] it is reiterated by many mystics, religious writers, and scholars of survival. Yogi Ramacharaka predicts:

> [The afterlife] shall be a reflection of the ideas and desires held by them during their period of earth life—a dramatization of their desire-ideals of their past life. In short, the Indian really finds his "happy hunting grounds," and the other primitive peoples their particular paradises as pictured in their creeds and faiths. . . . The conception of the "golden gates" is but a little higher in the scale than that of the "happy hunting ground" for it is purely material, and reflects the ideals of a race whose desires are for glittering and costly things.[5]

This argument might have interesting consequences for the nonbeliever: "The convinced materialist could experience the total emptiness they anticipated after death; the only essential difference would be that he finds himself still psychically living and conscious."[6]

This makes for a very neat theory indeed, with an ironic tinge of cosmic justice to it: if the materialists believe in meaninglessness and emptiness at death, that is just what they shall find.

This proposal might be reworked to square with empirical studies, but as it stands it is premature. For there are reports of near death experiences in which convinced materialists and atheists had "heavenly," mind opening experiences on their deathbeds. And there are devout religious people who die in agony and report nothing, or who experience only unconsciousness while being temporarily pronounced dead.[7]

It still might be true on some subtle level that "we experience what we believe" at death, but it is clear that belief in a certain species of afterlife alone is not adequate to produce that experience during the process of death. Yet it is reasonable to expect that the psychic state of people at death strongly influences their subsequent conscious experiences, if they have any.[8] In the popular Buddhist mind, however, the most widely expected postmortem state is one of reincarnation—either in a physical body here on this earth, or in a paraphysical body in another world.

Reincarnation

Regardless of the emotional ease or difficulty with which Western readers may respond to this concept, the Buddhist version of rebirth has been shown to be a reasonable hypothesis to explain verifiable memories of former lives. When a girl exhibits memories that could only be attributed to an old man now dead, and insists that she was that person before he died; when she shows skills and talents (linguistic, athletic, artistic) that she could not have learned in her present life and that the old man had had; and when, at the same time, marks on her body correspond to marks on the body of the deceased, then no other hypothesis can fit the data as well as taking the child's claim at almost face value.[9] There is a sense in which she was someone else in a former life on this earth, and now she is as she appears. Under carefully controlled conditions, cases of possession or hypnotic regression may provide similar evidence. On the basis of such combined evidence, it is most reasonable to accept that at least some people are reborn in new human bodies after their deaths in former human bodies. Theologian John Hick concludes:

> There are forms of reincarnation doctrine which may be broadly true pictures of what actually happens. It may be true, as Vedantist teaching claims, that an eternal "soul" or "higher self" lies behind a long series of incarnations. . . . Or it may be true, as Buddhist teaching claims, that "units" or "packages" of karma (as distinguished from higher selves) produce a series of persons, one of whom is me.[10]

Hick believes that persons do not evolve through a series of pre-human incarnations, but are created ab initio and ex nihilo by God. Either case is possible, but the evolutionary one is easier to square with scientific cosmology. Hick has also mentioned the debate between the Buddhists and Vedantins about what it is that survives bodily death. This debate becomes less of a problem in later Buddhism, and we can suggest at least one sense in which it is a pseudoproblem that need not trouble us further.

Resolving the Identity Problem

If a girl named Z remembers being an old man named Y who is now dead, it is trivially true that Z is not absolutely identical to Y. But then Z today is not identical to Z at birth. Whether we call Y the *same* as Z depends partly on the way we define sameness. The empirically verifiable fact is that there are people who identify themselves with previous people where such identification makes the best sense of their unusual memories, talents, and features. The important element here (in addition to memory) is that of continuity. This conscious continuity is preserved by the mental element that persists through various bodily sequences—called the ātman by Vedanta, and the alāya-vijñāna by Mahayana Buddhism. Both philosophies agree that the body is more temporary and less important than the cultivation of the mind. The Vedantin de-emphasizes the possessive grasping desires of the self by distinguishing between the empirical self, or *ahamkāra*, and the transcendental self, or true ātman, which does not really belong to any psychophysical personality in the first place. The Buddhist de-emphasizes the self in slightly different language, by saying that "there is no soul" (anattā), but recognizing a psychophysical personality built up of the five khandhās, and an element of consciousness that continues after the break up of the human personality and its components. The Vedantin may have a stronger sense of the integrity and individuality of the person, while the Buddhist emphasizes the constancy of change in the realm of phenomena.

"Laws" of Reincarnation

Although empirical studies are still in their infancy, the past twenty years of research have led to some further generalizations about the nature of rebirth, worthy of summarizing here:

1. Story's Law suggests that humans are usually reborn within a few hundred miles of their deaths, although not necessarily in territory known to the dying person.[11]
2. Evans-Wentz's Law says that persons will reincarnate in ways they believe possible; if people are raised to believe that sex change is impossible in rebirth, they will be reborn in bodies of the same sex, whereas if they believe sex change to be the normal pattern, that is what they will experience.[12]
3. Parker's Law sees violent death and unfulfilled cravings or desires for things in this life as the primary causes of reincarnation. (Both Stevenson and Banerjee have found that many of the reincarnation cases reported were those of people who had died violent deaths.) This corresponds with Buddhist teachings on the subject.[13]
4. Martinus' Law asserts that people are reborn relatively quickly when they die in childhood, but adults who die must spend a longer period in some intermediate state.[14] In fact, Stevenson's data suggest that periods of several years are not at all uncommon between remembered incarnations.[15]

We must stress that all of these "laws" or hypotheses are inductive generalizations open to empirical verification in the same way that generalizations about meteorites or earthquakes can be better confirmed or rejected as more and more examples are found and examined. However, we have no validated cases of people who report seeing their way into a new body at the very moment of death. The rebirth process, whether of days or of years, is not immediately apparent to dying persons as they depart from this world. As both Buddhist and empirical accounts have stressed, it is rather the element of consciousness which continues and is necessary to make sense of identity between rebirths. A process of consciousness alone is not enough, however, because if it stops thinking it stops existing.

So if we are to make any sense of personal identity at all, there must be both the process of consciousness and its ontological substrate present during this interim between incarnations. This locus of consciousness may be a vehicle or blueprint invisible to the human eye.[16] But it must exist, for if not, we have only the paradoxical situation of paranormal memories and replicated bodies with no genuinely real memories of past lives. Conversely, the existence of subtle bodies or ideal realms wherein consciousness might temporarily exist in a nonphysical state make meaningful the possibilities of resurrection and/or reincarnation, as well as other forms of survival.

An Ethereal Astral World

A discarnate body theory is the easiest way to make sense of individual identity and continuity of personality after death.[17] This theory would suggest that people have two bodies: a physical, material body, and an invisible, ethereal, or astral body. On this theory, the ethereal body leaves the corpse at death, as it may do temporarily during OBEs. Sometimes it appears to loved ones in other locations as if to inform them of the death or counsel them on some matter of importance to the deceased. Far from invalidating the theory, this problem of spirits bears directly on the problem of human destiny after death.[18] Nor need such a theory of invisible bodies conflict with modern science. Such bodies might well evolve through processes paralleling the evolution of our physical bodies from lower animals.[19] They may be the sorts of entities so commonly encountered in

Indian literature as the *linga sharīra* or the Buddhist ālaya-vijñāna—a subtle body of consciousness.[20]

Such a theory of normally invisible bodies might be made completely compatible with modern non-Newtonian physics, for "even the grossest materialism would have to allow that it is conceivable that the seat of consciousness and personality is not the physical brain after all but an 'astral' brain that can survive the death of the physical body."[21]

Some materialists might desire to disagree with this statement, but their disagreement would be based upon the faulty assumption that modern science has identified and understood everything in the universe. In fact, ours is only one body of knowledge in a long history of knowledge systems that have needed continual revision. "We are never entitled to declare that a certain effect must be non-physical just because it happens to be incompatible with any certain system of physics."[22]

The Brain as Filter

Many philosophers believe that our brains might be inherently capable of receiving more information than they do, but that the opacity of our senses to other phenomena has practical value. Kant reasoned that the body was not the cause of our thinking, but rather a condition restrictive of it.[23] In his essay entitled "Human Immortality," James developed the idea that the brain was a restrictive filter on reality.[24] Building on Bergson's ideas, Moncrieff put the theory of sense limitation into an evolutionary context: "The function of the sense organs is to restrict or canalize the clairvoyant powers which every sentient organism has, and to limit them . . . by shutting out what is biologically irrelevant."[25]

This may be one reason that we cannot normally see the subtle images which primitives and schizophrenics claim to see, or sense the myriad psychic impulses that may be whirling around us. Our brains shield us from them because they are not conducive to our effective functioning in this material world. The evidence on OBEs and apparitions in particular suggests that subtle bodies might exist and play a part in survival. Harrison proposes that

> Apparition bodies . . . have the advantage of not being visible to everybody, which could explain why we cannot see people in heaven or hell. Since apparitions do not exclude material objects from the space which they appear to occupy, there would be no difficulty about finding room for them. . . . This suggests the possibility of a community of people with apparition bodies communicating by auditory apparition words or apparition gestures.[26]

The existence of such realms is similarly asserted by Hindus and Buddhists. An apparitional survival world or worlds might contain bodylike structures, images, memory, and continuity. Thus it might make sense of survival in a way that even materialists could not reject.

Mind and Body

A couple of cautionary observations are in order here. First, the existence of subtle matter or fields does not in itself simplify the mind/body problem. For consciousness is not identical to its invisible body, if it has one, and we are still faced with the unanswerable question of their interaction, as C. D. Broad realized:

> There are plenty of fairly well-attested facts which afford prima facie empirical evidence of the ghost in the machine theory, if ghost is used in its proper sense . . . astral traveling, out-of-the-body experiences, haunting, bilocation, materialization, etc. . . . We shall then have to consider, in the case of each living person, two relationships, viz., (1) the relation of his mind to its

ghostly or astral body, and (2) the relation of the latter to his ordinary, physical body.[27]

Although astral-type bodies are a significant conceptual contribution to the survival question, they in no way solve the traditional mind/body problem. This is a humbling realization. We are still far from knowing much about the association of consciousness and the body. Although bodies may be used by humans to identify one another, and they provide convenient domains in which we can interact, it would be just as wrong to reduce humanhood to an astral body as to a physical body.[28] Thus, ethereal survival is not very meaningful unless it is somehow fundamentally mental.

Moreover, the existence of an astral body is still inadequate as a description of conscious survival. As H. D. Lewis has pointed out, the assurance that his astral body would continue to exist is as of little comfort as the assurance that his bones would not deteriorate. As long as astral bodies are not themselves equal to consciousness but are merely carriers of it, they do not guarantee the sort of survival that Buddhists seek. It is equally possible that, like corpses, some astral bodies continue for some time without continuing consciousness. It is the conscious aspects of the astral body that are important to survival, not the astral body by itself.

Studies of OBEs and apparitions provide some indications that their structures are fundamentally mental in some deeper sense than are our bodies. People reporting their OBEs, for example, say that their mere volition was able to effect performance of the action desired. Apparitions may appear fully clad within locked rooms. What provides this clothing is surely not the existence of ethereal hats and boots, but the power of the mind of the projector (cf. the case where a war widow sees her husband before her, dying in his bloody fatigues).[29] Thus there is a sense in which the subtle or apparitional realm is more psychically malleable, more open to direct volitional influence than our present physical universe appears to be.

An Ideational Next World

We have seen that Pure Land Buddhists affirm the ideational existence of the Pure Land, and the Tibetans of the bardo, or intermediate state. When we consider apparitions and OBEs, we find that their fully-clad character, their ability to move by volition alone, and their apparent transcendence of space, point also towards a more idealistic than materialistic view of things. Characteristics of NDEs such as visions of religious figures and heavenly realms also tend to indicate that the dying person is seeing into another state from which our senses normally shelter us, and which has some superphysical or idealistic ontological status. There is but a hazy grey line between asserting that there are other paraphysical dimensions like ours that behave in a more mental way, and asserting that there are realms of spirit and ideas as well as of matter. This is an old philosophical bone of contention that we need not resolve here. However, we can begin to study how Buddhist idealism would square with the concepts of science, how Buddhist idealism might be experimentally verifiable, and how we may resolve some of the problems which superficially appear to infect any Buddhist idealistic doctrine of survival.[30]

There need be no inherent conflict between the structure or existence of an idealistically based Buddhist next world and this. Aquinas' models of an image world experienced after death constitute one clear example of what the idealists' next world could be like; the heavens described by Pure Land Buddhists and by NDE patients give complementary pictures. To be meaningful, any sense of survival in a next world must include consciousness and perhaps memory and volition as primary characteristics. The physical body will not live after death, and we have seen that even an astral body living after death will be quite meaningless unless it is intimately associated with consciousness. Since it is the mind or consciousness whose survival we are considering, it need not surprise us that the realms of which it is conscious after the decease of the physical body are also mind dependent, or idealistic. Many thinkers have supported this suggestion.

Tyrrell and Ellis, among others, have argued that idealism makes the best sense of other worlds in their relation to this world.[31] Mundle and Beloff cogently argue that if ESP evidence counts in favor of dualism, then it counts even more strongly for Berkeley's forms of idealism in which there is no problem of how minds interact with matter at all, since matter is merely certain kinds of ideas in mind, and mind to mind interaction is taken as fundamental.[32] Murphy has found that even physicists are coming closer to the acceptance of a Berkeleyan idealism,[33] and this claim is at least superficially substantiated by LeShan's surveys.[34] In accounting for the objects of NDE visions, Ring reaches similar conclusions:

> Just where do the landscapes, the flowers, the physical structures, and so forth come from? In what sense are they "real"? . . . This is a realm that is created by interacting thought structures. . . . Since individual minds "create" this world (out of thoughts and images), this reality reflects to a degree the "thought-structures" of individuals used to the world of physical reality. . . . "The world of light" is indeed a mind-created world fashioned of interacting (or interfering) thought patterns. Nevertheless, that world is fully as real-seeming as is our physical world.[35]

In sum, the idea that the next world has idea-based images and perceptions receives some support from psychologists as well as Buddhist philosophers and NDE researchers. All agree that such an idealism makes consistent sense, both of the mechanisms of various psychic phenomena and of the scenery visualized in the next world during NDEs. Such an idealism, of course, is also in keeping with the suggestions of meditators and mystics in both Western and Eastern traditions.[36]

Such predictions of an idealistic next world need not conflict with the physicists' conceptions of this world, since they are ontologically distinct realms. But how could we ever know that the next world is in fact idealistic? Are such claims subject to the sorts of verification/falsification principles that we want to apply to statements about this world?

The confirmation of the idealist nature of the next world is not as impossible as the question might presuppose. If Buddhists are correct that mystic meditation gives previews of the same realms that are visible at death, then we need not wait until death but can conduct other sorts of research with living meditating subjects.[37] Further investigations of OBEs and NDEs may yield additional facts which tend to confirm or deny the idealist hypothesis. Of course, we might have to devise new methodologies of science to investigate a realm which is in essence experienceable but mind dependent and nonmaterial.

The one scientist to take this proposal seriously is Charles Tart. He has suggested that we should recognize Altered States of Consciousness (ASCs) as giving insights into other idealistic realities. Tart advocates research using teams of people who would volunteer to explore the realms of the mind much as we now explore the sea or the stratosphere. They would be trained in methods of reporting and objectivity, and would learn to verbally report experiences as they were having them, or to remember them in such ways that they could be recorded immediately on return to waking consciousness and this world. They could be given carefully controlled doses of drugs which are known to produce ASCs, or could rely solely on their natural meditative abilities to achieve altered states if they showed talents in that direction.

Tart knows that the public is not receptive to such proposals at the moment, and he is well aware of the dangerous side effects of some hallucinogens. Philosophically, the important point is that we can make a cogent case for the scientific study of ideational realms through altered states of mind. Whether Tart's program is adopted or not, its canons and principles harmonize with those of modern science.[38]

If a program like Tart's were ever adopted, we might gradually learn what psychological, religious, and physical variables contribute to enabling or producing what visions, and how we can better compare the visions of different subjects. It might even become possible to take intersubjective trips in which two or more people experience themselves going together to another realm, just as it is possible to have shared dreams. The important point is that such meditative or altered state access to idealistic realms might give verification to statements about the status and contents of such realms. Thus, the statement that the next world is an idea-based realm is in principle verifiable, and not subject to positivist charges of unfalsifiability and hence meaninglessness.

That we should be able to construct a geography of idealistic landscapes, while mind boggling to many Westerners, is nothing new to Asia. To name but a few, Patanjali's Yoga system, the *Visudhimagga* of the Abhidharmists, the *Meditation Sutra* of the Pure Land Sects, and the *Book of the Dead*, are step-by-step guides to achieving other states and experiencing other realms, with the assumption that the practitioner will be able to verify for himself the teachings through discipline and practice.[39]

Impersonal Transcendental States

If there is some sort of depersonalized, transcendental, nirvanalike state in which memory and volition as well as bodies are eradicated, there might be more serious reason to ask whether such survival were truly personal. It might be personal in the sense that a stream of consciousness might continue distinct from other streams of consciousness. Yet without memory or volition, such minds might not merit the label of "person" in the way we are accustomed to using the term. Such arguments do not in any way diminish the likelihood of such states existing. Rather, they make such a prospect simply more or less appealing according to one's religious predilections, and they approach the boundaries of the indiscussible.

If the body and brain are filters on reality, and if such filters do not continue after bodily death, it is possible that death may represent the end of all personal limits and boundaries without necessarily being the end of conscious experience altogether. A radical removal of the limitations of consciousness might lead either to a sense of union with a collective unconscious, to an explosion or expansion of consciousness into transpersonal states, or into other states of disembodied consciousness difficult to depict or identify. This theory is defended most adamantly by Michael Grosso, but C. D. Broad also speculated about the khandhā-like break up of the personality into floating bits of psychic flotsam and jetsam at death.[40] Murphy sometimes shared this view, but felt that it would change the whole nature of survival discussion:

> Does personality survive bodily death or not? The question presupposes a sharpness, a distinctness, an encapsulation which simply is not an attribute of the thing we know as personality. . . . Human personality during life here on earth is an aspect of the field in which it appears. After death the field must surely be very different. No fixed unit recognizable in one field can be transferred, as by surgical implantation [to another].[41]

Grosso, Broad, and Murphy expect the depersonalization of mind at death as an inevitable consequence of the loss of bodily restrictions. Price and Hick, by contrast, also recognize the possibility of transcendent nirvanic states after death, but deny that they will be automatic; rather, they must be achieved after much further spiritual development. Hick concludes his massive study of survival with the prediction: "In progressively 'higher' worlds . . . self-protective egoity withers away, so that the individual's series of lives culminates in a last life beyond which there is no further embodiment but instead entry into the common Vision of God, or nirvāna, or the eternal consciousness of the ātman in its relation to Ultimate Reality."[42]

Studies of NDEs suggest that few if any people realize a nirvanic transcendence of all personal consciousness at the very moment of death, although a decrease in ego boundaries is occasionally mentioned. Buddhist theory would propose that true nirvana is accessible only to the most spiritual of persons. It is possible that some people like the Buddha realized such a state immediately upon death, and that other arhats or bodhisattvas achieved it after existing temporarily in some other postmortem state.

Grosso says that the concept of indescribable nirvanic states has been ignored in the West because of its unpalatability to traditional Christians—but palatability has nothing to do with its truth.[43] The worst problem with such states is not so much that they are hard to accept as that they are hard to explain. This is one reason that the Buddha remained silent when asked about his existence after death.

In more modern phrasing, if we know that Jones will transcend personality but still have some sense of consciousness after death, can we call that consciousness which survives Jones? Murphy responds that this sort of question itself contains illegitimate presuppositions. In short, a nirvanalike state may well exist, but if it does, it is not something which we can very fruitfully discuss in ordinary language—nor is the question of personal survival any longer a meaningful question in that context. The person is neither immortalized nor destroyed. There is no more self, but the consciousness is not thereby necessarily annihilated.

Possible Afterlife Scenarios

The variety inherent both in the human condition and in human experiences of death implies that not all persons should be expected to experience the same thing (if anything at all) at death. Let us here imagine a range of conceivable possibilities after death:

1. Some people lack coherent conscious experience after being pronounced dead. Many other people report nothing after being revived from a coma. While there may be some problems in memory or hesitation in reporting, the evidence suggests that for some people, at least, death may simply be a blackout—the end.

2. Some people are reborn into other human bodies. They are most likely to remember their former lives if their deaths were violent and if their culture does not suppress such reports. Except for cases in which young children are reborn there will normally be a period of years intervening between reincarnations. In rare instances, reincarnation may also take the forms of spirit possession or be revealed by hypnotic regression. But no one reports being reborn at the moment of death.

3. Some people will survive in ethereal astral bodies after the decay of their physical bodies. They are the gods and ghosts of Mahayana Buddhism. The fact that most apparitions of living people are produced by the people they resemble suggests that most apparitions of the dead are also produced by the people they resemble. This case is strengthened by the fact that apparitions sometimes convey information or motivations known only to the deceased. Apparitions are most intelligible on the assumption that there are other forms of matter, fields, or dimensions which physics has not yet studied. To any persons surviving in ethereal bodies it will feel as if their loci of conscious thought and perception had been released

from their heads at death, and they were now living in continuing out-of-body experiences.

4. Some people will find themselves passing away into realms which are ideational or idealistic in their ontology. While some of the scenery and images perceived in such states will be unique to each individual, other features may be intersubjectively perceived by many consciousnesses. Such idealistic realms need feel no less physical for their lack of material substrate or their violation of laws of matter. The idealist model best accounts for the phenomena of Mahayana meditative and deathbed visions.

5. At some point after death, some people may experience selfless transpersonal or transcendent (nirvanic) states. Since they are superpersonal, they go beyond the present discussion of personal survival, and we lack the appropriate language and experience to characterize such states further.

In each of these cases, we are talking only about survival shortly after the death of the physical body. None of this should be taken to rule out the possibility of a worldwide resurrection, judgment, and conditionalist immortality a thousand years hence on a Christian model. But unless some of our conclusions are true, God's resurrection of new people would be only a great day of replica making, for there will be no conscious continuity nor personal identity unless some survival of types 2 to 4 is admitted.

The entire array of afterlives (2 to 5) above is closely compatible with the worldview of Mahayana and Vajrayāna Buddhism. In these Buddhist traditions, there is both rebirth of people into this world (2), and also rebirth into the invisible realms of ghosts or gods (3). In addition, there is passage through a tube or vortex to idealistic realms (4), whose essential structure is ideational and may be experienced in meditation as well as at death. Finally, for the rare Buddha or bodhisattva, there may be a state of selfless nirvana at death (5), of which we can say no more.

The fourfold view of the next world concluded above is more consistent with experience and more philosophically insightful than is mechanistic billiard ball materialism, to which large sectors of the "educated" community still dogmatically cling. In the measured phrasing of philosopher C. J. Ducasse: "The balance of the evidence so far obtained is on the side of the reality of survival, and in the best cases, of survival not merely of life on earth, but survival also of the most significant capacities of the human mind, and of the continuing exercise of these."[44]

Ducasse arrived at these conclusions after careful studies of his own thirty years ago. The best evidence for survival has just emerged in the NDE research of the past fifteen years, and it fully supports his judgment. Both the Buddha and many modern scientists would agree on this conclusion. There remain some issues which are particularly important for future studies to confirm or falsify, and which may affect our conclusions here.

We do need more extensive and rigorous studies of NDEs, particularly with regard to physical states and cultural influences. Further reporting of NDEs and proof of brain death prior to resuscitation is important to set straight the widespread popular impression that experience of any kind is impossible without cranial activity. Such studies might literally prove at least temporary survival, and utterly refute the already obsolescent mind/brain identity theory. Comparative studies of atheists, Buddhists, and unlettered jungle tribespeople may also give us important data on how universal deathbed visions really are, and how much a product of cultures which more or less consciously believe and expect them.

We also need a deeper understanding of meditative states of consciousness. Whether meditative states give perspectives into other realities or merely image the psychological state of the subject, there is much to be learned from such research. Perhaps Tart's plan for universities or laboratories of people pooling, comparing, and analyzing their findings on meditative states may someday become a reality. Then we shall learn much more about the nonphysical geographies of the minds in which we live. In the meantime, we still have the chance to explore such realms individually, preferably under the careful supervision of trained masters.

The question of personal survival of physical death is actually the question of the nature of humanhood, the relations of consciousness to reality, and to the body with which it normally seems affiliated. One in ten people may give us usable evidence about the nature of survival on their deathbeds—once in their lifetime. If Buddhists and mystics are correct that glimpses of other realities including the afterlife may be gained through disciplined meditations in this life, then this offers us another course worthy of investigation. It is a pathway which may be practiced and evaluated on its own merits, even as the Buddha urged his followers to do.

The Afterlife and Rewards for Goodness

Some readers will doubtless be disappointed that overt connections have not been drawn between the nature of the afterlife and the ways we live in this world. Others will feel that the most important arguments for an afterlife are ethical ones to which we have scarcely alluded in this work: that conceptions of future life are essential to assure that there is cosmic justice in the universe.

To deal with the latter issue first: it is by no means clear that the universe is just, that there is any sense in which the universe must be just, or indeed that it would necessarily be any more just if there were an afterlife. Such ethically motivated arguments may persuade the already religious, they may make us long for a realm where present sufferings will be recompensed and wrongs will be righted, they may imbue the cosmos with a sense of meaning for humans that a nonethical universe would lack. But they give us no irrefutable insights into the nature of things. It is possible that the universe is not the way we think that it ought to be, and we must be as wary of arguing from "ought" to "is" as we are of arguing from "is" to "ought."

To the former question—the ethical relevance of survival to this present world—we must regretfully respond that there is too little evidence to make any statement. We are in a position ironically similar to that of the Buddha (who saw good men born into both good and bad wombs, and evil men born into both good and bad wombs), but we are not yet able to sort out all the factors and variables as he was reputed to have done. We do have evidence that many nonreligious people have heavenly NDEs, and occasionally very devout people have hellish ones. People who would be judged equally moral by most human standards have extremely different experiences at death, ranging from blackout or life review to OBE or beatific visions. Either our moral judgments are terribly faulty, or there is no correspondence between moral status and NDEs, or both. We simply do not know enough to predict which actions or beliefs will lead to what sorts of experiences, so we are in no position to make moralistic pronouncements.

"However," someone might argue, "if there is even a fair chance that consciousness may survive, we should cultivate our minds, which will be more lasting, rather than seeking first material goods, status, wealth, etc." While Buddhists are in strong sympathy with this statement, we should probably feel the same even if there were no evidence for survival.

This is not to deny that survival is an issue of immense ethical importance. It may cause us to rethink the ways we look at euthanasia, suicide, and the right to die, as the concluding chapter will attempt to do. Many wise Buddhists in many cultures have stressed that there *is* a moral nature to the universe, and that we will more clearly discern this in our next lives. If so, this too has very important implications for how we live and think here and now. But like the question of idealism, this too is an issue for personal choice and faith.

7

Buddhist
Ethics of
Death and Dying

Death, Dying, and Bioethics in Japan

RESEARCH ON DEATH is receiving a lot of attention in the West these days. Some universities have designed new programs in death education or Thanatology. Books on death and dying have become bestsellers. Newspapers and television programs frequently highlight the subject. In Japan as well as America, this interest is due to the modernization and sterilization of the dying process. In the old days, people used to die at home, surrounded by their loved ones. Today, people die surrounded only by machines, tubes, and masked nurses in modern hospitals.

One unexpected by-product of the new scientification of the

dying process is that some patients revive after nearly dying or even after being pronounced dead. Many of them report having unusual experiences while their minds are "out of their bodies." Of course there are problems in the analysis and interpretation of these NDEs. But their widespread nature has led Western scholars to begin rethinking the nature of the dying process. Many scholars even believe that such research can enable us to catch a glimpse of the beginning of the next world, or afterlife. Moreover, as a patient's last hours are increasingly controlled by doctors, more and more modern people are beginning to request procedures which will enable death with dignity.

Issues of terminal care, euthanasia, and organ transplantation are no longer unique to the Euro-American world. Advances in medical technology have forced Japan, China, and other traditionally Buddhist countries to ask questions about the meaning of human life and determination of human death. Until recently, oriental doctors with training only in Western medicine have paternalistically made most such decisions for their patients, but a growing discontent with this paternalism is being felt. It is not that the doctors consciously reject Buddhism, but that their training has been totally Western. Few Buddhists have come forth to propose alternative criteria for medical ethics in Asia.

Japanese Buddhist scholars have been slow to address contemporary issues of bioethics, suicide, and death with dignity. Although the practical problems are frequently addressed in the popular press and scattered citizens groups are beginning to draw attention to them, few people outside of the medical community have seriously confronted the issues.[1] The prolonged hospitalization and extreme procedures used to keep the unconscious Showa Emperor (Hirohito) alive focused Japanese attention on bioethical issues in medicine. A recent annual meeting of the Japan Ethics Association was entitled "Life and Ethics." Ostensibly, this as a chance to promote discussion between medical, philosophical and Buddhist bioethicists. In fact, only a few Japanese scholars have attempted to put forth Buddhist views on bioethics, particularly euthanasia and death with dignity.

The majority of ethicists at the Association seemed to agree with Anzai Kazuhiro's presentation that brain death should not be equated with human death.[2] Anzai's reasoning runs as follows: If brain death implies human death, then by contraposition, human life must imply conscious (brain) life. Now there are clearly segments of our lives in which we are alive but not always conscious. Therefore, it is wrong to conclude that a human is dead because he or she lacks consciousness.

Although widely heard in Japan, Anzai's argument has at least two logical problems. First, it fails to recognize the key criterion of irreversibility. Some periods of unconsciousness (like deep sleep) have an expectation of future revival, whereas other types of unconsciousness (like irreversible coma) have no expectation of future revival. This question of irreversibility is precisely the distinction upon which we must decide whether or not to attempt to resuscitate a patient, and how long to prolong treatment of the patient's unconscious body. So the fact that there are some times when we are unconscious (asleep) but alive does not imply that every time we are unconscious we are also alive. Anzai is correct that "it is wrong to conclude that a human is dead because he or she lacks consciousness," but he is incorrect to imply that lack of consciousness can never be an indication of death.

Anzai argues that there are times when people are alive even when their brains are not active. Later, he undercuts his own argument here by sometimes collapsing brain life and conscious life. He treats brain and consciousness as the same, but says people are sometimes alive even without brain or consciousness. It would be more Buddhist to argue that brain and consciousness are not the same because there are times when the brain is active but consciousness is not, and there may be times when consciousness is active when the brain is not (as in certain meditative states). Then Anzai would have a stronger basis for arguing that brain death should not be treated as death of the person. But his position is representative of a widely seen Japanese rejection of brain-death criteria.

This problem is partly based on the difference between Christian and Buddhist views of human life. In dualist Christian tradition, a person is mysteriously composed of two dissimilar elements, spirit (mind) and matter. When the spirit leaves the body at death, the body becomes no more than material refuse, a corpse, and can be disposed of accordingly. Apart from sentimental memories, there is nothing sacred about a dead body itself. The sacred essence of human existence is the soul, which is no longer within the body after death. Thus the irreversible termination of consciousness, correlating with the departure of the soul from the body, signals the point at which the body is no longer a person and can be treated as a thing. In other words, after brain death, a body is no longer a person and need not be treated as one.

The Japanese Buddhist view, however, is more holistic. The body is as much a part of personhood as is the mind. In traditional Japan, as in Tibet, death was understood to be a long process, not an instant of determination. Even after a patient's consciousness seemed to drift away and pupils dilated, a time was set aside for various religious activities. Food would be prepared and placed at the bedside of the dead person. As the dead person showed no reaction to the food, the family would call out the name of the deceased from the rooftop or from the garden well, summoning the spirit. If this produced no reaction, then the pillow might be kicked out from under the corpse's head (*makura hazushi*) or other mild violence practiced around it. Only when there was no response to all these activities (often after an hour or more), would the person be pronounced "departed" (*gorinju*).

Even after being pronounced departed, the body is treated as an honored body (*goitai*), not as a corpse (*shitai*). It is bathed, shaved, dressed, greeted, and treated in many respects like a living but dependent person for several days, from the time of pronouncement of death, through the wake, until the delivery to the morgue or crematorium. During this period, there are in fact rare cases when honored bodies actually revive and come back to life.

More importantly, in Japanese society persons are not independent individual entities. They exist only as nodes within nexuses of personal relationships. Decisions are not made by individuals in a vacuum, but by groups of people considering their mutual interactions. Even when persons are physically dead, the groups of people gathered at their wakes are united by their relationships to and their concerns for the deceased. The deceased persons remain at the center of their decision-making networks, uniting their concerns and influencing their decisions as effectively as if they were alive but simply asleep or absent. Insofar as the person-centered decision-making group still functions conscious of the dead person's wishes, there is a sense in which the dead person is still alive.

From the Japanese perspective, the Western medical viewpoint conflates several important points of passage into one instant. In the Japanese view, there is first (1) the time at which a patient may be clinically determined to be brain dead, (2) the time at which the consciousness is no longer present in the body, (acknowledging that consciousness may hang around a body or place even after the brain is inactive), (3) the time at which a patient is actually pronounced dead, and preparations for the funeral begin, and (4) the time from which a dead person is treated as a thing or corpse, to be cremated or otherwise disposed of. The Western view collapses all of these into a single instant, the time when the patient is pronounced dead and is no longer a person. Even if there are some medical reasons for this practice, it may have adverse psychological effects in not allowing affected people enough time to digest the news or appropriately deal with their emotions. So the Japanese reasoning is based both on tradition and sound psychological practice, as well as on logical distinctions worthy of further study.

Buddhism and the Acceptance of Death

In his keynote address about Buddhist ethics, Reverend Kawasaki Shinjō explained that Japanese rejection of brain death criteria may also be grounded in a Buddhist view of life and death.[3] He cited the *Visuddhimagga*, which indicates that life energy (*ayus*) is supported by body warmth and conscious faculties (broadly interpretable to include reflexes).[4] If either body heat or reflexes remain, then a person cannot be considered dead.

Now Buddhism further admits situations (such as hypothermia and meditative trances) in which body warmth or reflexes may not be externally detectable but the subject is not yet dead. So lack of warmth and reflexes is a necessary but not sufficient indicator of death; if either persists, it can be said that the body is not yet dead. In other words, Buddhism does not equate life with warmth and reflexes, but holds that body heat and reflexes are the supports of life, and therefore life cannot be empirically measurable except through such variables.

Kawasaki also reaffirms the widespread Japanese Buddhist view that death is not the end of life, but merely a brief transition to another state, commonly thought to last for forty-nine days, which occurs between life in this body and life in the next. The reluctance to dismiss a body as dead prior to its loss of warmth and reflexes is not based on a fear of personal extinction or annihilation, but rather on a Buddhist view of the basic components of the life system.[5] Chiba's Iida Tsunesuke expands this view by arguing that "persons are not merely the meaningless 'subjects of rights,' but personalities, 'faces' embodying the possibilities of fulfilling the dreams of their parents or loved ones . . . recipients of love, and therefore worthy of honoring."[6]

Logically speaking, the so-called possibilities argument has long ago been laid to rest by philosophers like Mary Anne Warren, who demonstrated that we need not treat potential presidents as presidents, potential criminals as criminals, or potential humans as humans.[7] (Japanese society might differ in this respect; until recently, suspicion of a crime or likelihood of committing a crime was sufficient grounds for arrest, and children of nobles (potential lords) were often honored or killed as real lords.)[8]

However, Iida's argument is less important for its logical persuasion than for its revelation of the Japanese attitude: persons are not subjects with rights and individual free wills, but rather objects of the attentions of others. Japanese treatment of infants and children reinforces this view, for Japanese children are seen not as persons but as possessions of their parents; this was the legal as well as philosophical status of women and servants as well as children prior to the twentieth century.

This position is further developed by Ōhara, who argues that "although a body may be treated as a 'thing' or a corpse by physicians, it remains a body of value and meaning, and in that sense, a person, to members of its family. . . . In this sense, even vegetative humans and brain-dead corpses can give joy to other people."[9] Of course it is only in the most metaphorical of senses that a corpse can give anything to anyone. Rather, it is the family who may derive some sense of joy by beholding the face of one dear to them, even though that person is incapable of ever being conscious in that body again.

This attitude is akin to the Japanese reverence for pictures, sculptures, and myths; it provides no useful guidelines whatsoever to the medical faculty as to when to continue or desist what kinds of treatment for the patient. To the question, "When does a body stop being a person?" the Ōharan answer, "It never stops being a person to those who love it," may be psychologically correct for some people. In the rare but increasing cases where old people die alone and uncared for, the absence of concerned others leaves the medical practitioner utterly without guidelines. This is consistent with the frequently noted proposition that Japanese without social contexts seem morally at a loss.[10]

Thus, the Japanese tradition values the person (or corpse) entirely in terms of his value to others. For many Japanese parents, children are indeed objects. In fact, there are rehabilitation hospitals in Japan in which anencephalic infants are cared for and raised for as many years as their parents' finances and interest dictate; they are propped up and made to "greet" their parents whenever the parents visit.[11]

However, unwillingness to admit the finality of death or the fundamental suffering of the human condition runs counter to the basic tenets of Buddhism. We are reminded of the famous story of the woman who asked the Buddha to revive her baby. In response, the Buddha instructed her to ask food of a house in which no one had died. In the process of asking around the entire village, the woman came to realize that all humans must die and deal with death. In this way she gained enlightenment, stopped grieving for her dead child, and became a follower of the Buddha. Thus, the relatives who refuse to pronounce another relative dead as long as she has a face, or the parents who insist on artificially prolonging the appearance of life of an anencephalic infant, cannot claim to understand Buddhism.

However, the Japanese rejection of brain-death criteria is related to the Japanese association of brain-death criteria with organ transplantation. Many Japanese continue to manifest a distaste for organ transplantation which dates back to Confucian teachings, which state that the body must be buried whole and never cut because it is a gift from heaven and from one's parents. For this reason, dissections and autopsies were late in coming to Japan, not widely permitted until the nineteenth century. The modern Japanese practices of universal cremation, of autopsies, of surgical operations, and of flying to other countries to have organ transplants, all have superseded the old

Confucian prejudice against body cutting. There remains a fear that if brain death criteria were widely accepted, less conservative elements of society might abuse it for the sake of the distasteful practice of organ transplantation.

The problem in Japanese society is that the adoption of a given practice by a group places great pressure on all persons to follow that practice as a norm. In other words, if it becomes standard practice for Japanese to leave their bodies to science or donate their organs upon death, then it will become almost impossible for anyone to decline this practice. Such organ donation might be a good thing, but at the same time the right of individual decision making must be preserved. The difficulty in Japanese society is that if society as a whole accepts something as a good thing, it then becomes terribly difficult for an individual to choose anything else.

The situation is further complicated by the fact that Japanese doctors are almost gods unto themselves, unchecked by fear of lawsuits or surveillance. If transplantation becomes a common practice, and if a recipient is in need of a certain organ which a potential donor near death might provide, it will become extremely easy and highly lucrative for the doctor to hasten the death of the donor in order to provide the needed organ in time. In the Japanese hospital situation, there is no danger that someone would dare to challenge a doctor's spurious declaration that a patient had died naturally. The absence of whistle-blowing in Japan renders Japanese doctors virtually immune from fear of retribution for hastening transplant operations.

The above discussion explains in part the slow growth of Japanese thought in bioethics, and particularly their concerns with bodies of value to others rather than with subjects of value to themselves. Although this concern finds no support either in Japanese Buddhism nor in samurai teaching, on the level of popular belief it may have serious ramifications for Japanese bioethics for many generations to come.

The World Federation of the Right to Die Society held an

International Conference in Nice, France in 1984. Although many Japanese attended this conference, apparently none of them contributed to the West's understanding of Buddhist views of euthanasia. When the President of the Society published a book on world attitudes on euthanasia the following year, only 2 percent (2.5 out of 150 pages) was about Buddhist attitudes, and those ideas were gained from California Buddhists, not from Japanese Buddhists at Nice.[12]

Early Buddhist Views of Suicide and Euthanasia

Japan has long been more aware of and sensitive to the dying process than modern Western cultures. Moreover, Japan already has its own good philosophical and experiential background to deal effectively with new issues of bioethics, such as euthanasia. Japanese Buddhists have long recognized what Westerners are only recently rediscovering: that the manner of dying at the moment of death is very important. This fundamental premise probably predates Buddhism itself, but it is also made very explicit in the teachings of the Buddha, as we observed earlier.[13]

In his meditations, the Buddha noticed that even people with good karma were sometimes born into bad situations, and even those with bad karma sometimes found inordinately pleasant rebirths. The Buddha declared that the crucial variable governing rebirth was the nature of the consciousness at the moment of death. Thereafter, Buddhists placed high importance on holding the proper thoughts at the moment of death. Many examples of this idea can be found in two works of the Theravāda canon, the *Petavatthu* and the *Vimānavatthu* ("Stories of the Departed"). Indeed, in many sutras, monks visit laymen on their death beds to ensure that their dying thoughts are wholesome,[14] and the Buddha recommends that lay followers similarly encourage each other on such occasions.[15]

Buddhism sees death as not the end of life, but simply as a transition, so suicide offers no escape from anything. In the early *sangha* (community of followers of the Buddha), suicide was in principle condemned as an inappropriate action.[16] But the early Buddhist texts include many cases of suicide that the Buddha himself accepted or condoned. For example, the suicides of Vakkali[17] and of Channa [18] were committed in the face of painful and irreversible sickness. It is significant however, that the Buddha's praise of these suicides is not based on the fact that they were in terminal states, but rather that their minds were selfless, desireless, and enlightened at the moments of their passing.

This theme is more dramatically visible in the example of Godhika. This disciple repeatedly achieved an advanced level of samadhi, bordering on embodied (sopadhisesa) nirvana, and then slipped out of the state of enlightenment into normal consciousness again. After this happened six times, Godhika at last vowed to pass on to the next realm while enlightened, and quietly suicided during the afterglow from his next period of samadhi. While cautioning his other disciples against suicide, the Buddha nonetheless blessed and praised Godhika's steadiness of mind and purpose, and declared that he had passed on to nirvana.

In short, the acceptability of suicide, even in the early Buddhist community, depended not on terminal illness alone, but upon the state of selfless equanimity with which one was able to pass away. It is interesting to note in passing that all these suicides were committed by the subject knifing himself, a technique which came to be standardized in later Japanese ritual suicide.

When asked about the morality of suiciding to move on to the next world, the Buddha did not criticize it.[19] He emphasized that only the uncraving mind would be able to move on towards nirvana, and that conversely, minds desiring to get something or to flee from something by their deaths might achieve nothing.

Similarly, there are stories in the *Jātaka* of the Buddha giving his own body (in former lives) to save other beings, both animals and humans. Thus, death out of compassion for others is also lauded in the scriptures.[20] It is also well known that in the Jain tradition, saints were expected to fast until their deaths,[21] and there have been those in both China and Japan who have followed this tradition thereafter.[22]

In China, it is believed that a disciple of Shan-tao's jumped out of a tree in order to kill himself and reach the Pure Land. Shan-tao's response was not that the action of suicide were right or wrong in and of itself, but that the disciple who wanted so strongly to see the Pure Land was doubtless ready to reach it.[23] Other more recent examples may be found in the Buddhist suicides by Vietnamese monks protesting the Vietnam government.[24] Whether these stories are all historical fact or not is not at issue here. The point is thatthey demonstrate the consistent Buddhist position towards suicide: There is nothing intrinsically wrong with taking one's own life, if not done in hate, anger, or fear. Equanimity or preparedness of mind is the main issue.

In summary, Buddhism realizes that death is not the end of anything, but a transition. Buddhism has long recognized persons' rights to determine when they should move on from this existence to the next. The important consideration here is not whether the body lives or dies, but whether the mind can remain at peace and in harmony with itself. The Jōdō (Pure Land) tradition tends to stress the continuity of life, while the Zen tradition tends to stress the importance of the time and manner of dying. Both of these ideas are deeply rooted in the Japanese consciousness.

Buddhist Suicide and Dignified Death in Japan

Japanese Buddhists traditionally demonstrated an unconcern with death even more than their neighbors. Japanese valued peace of mind and honor of life over length of life. While samurai often suicided on the battlefield or in court to preserve their dignity in death, countless commoners chose suicide in order to obtain a better future life in the Pure Land. On some occasions, whole masses of people suicided at the same time. In others, like the situation depicted in Kurosawa's famous film "Red Beard," poverty stricken families committed suicide in order to escape unbearable suffering in this life and find a better life in the world to come. Often parents would kill their children first and then kill themselves; this kind of double suicide of loved ones (*shinjū*) can still be seen in Japan today. The issue becomes: How does Buddhism appraise such suicide intended to gain heavenly rebirth?

On a popular level, the desire to "leave this dirty world and approach the Pure Land" (*enri edo, gongu jōdō*), was fostered by wandering itinerant monks such as Kūya in the Heian period and Ippen in the Kamakura period. The tradition of suiciding by entering a river or west-facing seashore apparently began in the Kumano area, but rapidly spread throughout the nation along with the Pure Land faith upon which it was based.[25]

The common tradition was to enter the water with a rope tied around one's waist and held by one's retainers or horse. If one's nerve and single-minded resolution failed, then one would not achieve rebirth in the Pure Land as desired. In this instance, either the suicide or his retainers (judging from his countenance) might stop the suicide attempt and save him from dying with inappropriate thoughts. However, if the suicide retained a peaceful and unperturbed mind and countenance throughout the drowning, the retainers were to let him die in peace, and simply retain his body for funeral purposes. Such situations clearly demonstrate that what is at stake here is not the individual's right to die, but rather his ability to die with peace of mind. If death with a calm mind is possible, then it is not condemned.

A paradigmatic example of this situation is found in the records of Saint Ippen.[26] Ajisaka Nyūdō, a Pure Land aspirant who was possibly of noble descent, gave up his home and family to follow the teachings of Saint Ippen. For unclear reasons, Ippen refused him admission to his band of itinerant mendicants, but advised him that the only way to enter the Pure Land was to die holding the name and figure of Amida in mind (*nembutsu*). Nyūdō then suicided by drowning himself in the Fuji River.

The scene is vividly depicted in the scroll paintings.[27] Nyūdō is seen with a rope around his waist. His attendants on the shore hold one end of the rope. As he bobs above the current, he is seen preserving the *gasshō* posture, perfectly at peace and in prayer. Music is heard from the purple clouds above him, a common sign of *ōjō* (rebirth in the Pure Land).

When Ippen heard of this suicide, he praised Nyūdō's faith, interpreting the purple clouds and Nyūdō's unruffled demeanor as proof of his attainment of rebirth in the Pure Land. At the same time, repeating Nyūdō's last words (*nagori wo oshimuna*), he warned his other disciples not to grieve at their master's passing.[28] When Ippen himself died, six of his disciples also suicided in sympathy, hoping to accompany their master to the Pure Land. This occasioned some debate about the propriety of sympathy suicide. Shinkyō, Ippen's leading disciple and second patriarch of the Ji School, declared that the disciples had failed to obtain rebirth in the Pure Land, for their action was seen as self-willed and Pure Land faith relies entirely on the power and will of Amida Buddha. Assertion of self-will is seen as running counter to the reliance on other power demanded by the Amida faith.[29] Several important points can be learned from these examples.

First, suicide is never condemned per se; it is the state of mind which determines the rightness or wrongness of the suicide situation. The division between choosing one's own time and place of death with perfectly assured peace of mind, and self-willing one's own death at the time of one's master's death is perhaps a hazy grey line. This should not obscure the criteria involved: death with desires does not lead to rebirth in the Pure Land, but death with calm assurance does. Even the method of water suicide using a rope as a preventive backup stresses the importance of the state of mind in this action.

Secondly, Nyūdō's famous phrase, *nagori wo oshimuna*, means that Buddhists are not to kill themselves in sympathy when others die. A literal translation would be that we are not to cling to what remains of the name or person, but to let them go freely on to the next world. In other words, when someone dies with an assured state of mind, it is not for those who remain either to criticize or to wish that he had not died in this situation. Those who are left behind are to respect and not resent, reject, or grieve for a death which might seem to them untimely.

It is not coincidental that the Japanese word for euthanasia is *anrakushi*, a term with many Buddhist meanings. In Buddhist terminology, *anrakukoku* is another name for *Jōdō*, the Pure Land, the next world of the Buddha Amida, to which each Japanese expects to go after death. German-educated doctor and historical novelist Mori Ōgai's famous book *Takasebune* specifically deals with anrakushi; it is the story of Yoshisuke killing his sickly young brother who wants to die but lacks the strength to kill himself.[30] Many famous twentieth-century Japanese authors wrote of suicide, and some, such as Akutagawa, Dazai, Kawabata, and Mishima, suicided themselves. Following the deaths of each emperor (even in recent years), faithful retainers have also suicided in sympathy with their departed leaders. While some of these suicides show un-Buddhist anger, pessimism, or nihilism, they are still reminders that the Japanese Buddhist worldview does not condemn suicide.

Japanese law does not criminalize suicide, and European law is slowly beginning to follow the Japanese model in this regard. However, Japanese law does hold it to be a crime to assist or encourage a suicide. In normal situations, this is only wise and prudent, for healthy people should be encouraged to live and make the most of their lives. But in the situations where death with dignity (*songenshi*) is requested, it is precisely because the person is facing imminent death that it is morally acceptable to assist the suicide, particularly if the motive is mercy.

Samurai Seppuku *and Euthanasia*

Among the warrior elite who usually followed Zen Buddhism, suicide was considered an honorable alternative to being killed by others or continuing a life in shame or misery. Beginning with the famous self-disemboweling of Minamoto no Tametomo and Minamoto no Yorimasa in 1170, *seppuku* became known as the way an honorable vanquished Buddhist warrior would end his life.[31] Soon thereafter, headed by Taira Noritsune and Taira Tomomori, hundreds of Taira warriors and families suicided in the battle of Dannoura of 1185. Famous suicides include that of Kusunoki Masashige in 1336 in the battle between Nitta and Hosokawa, and that of Toyotomi Hideyori under siege by the Tokugawas in 1615.

In the Tokugawa period, love suicides were dramatized in a dozen plays by Chikamatsu, such as *Sonezaki Shinjū, Shinjū Ten no Amijima,* and *Shinjū Mannensō*.[32] The forty-seven *Akō Rōshi*, who suicided after avenging their master's death, became another famous true story, dramatized in the *Chūshingura* plays and films.[33] The samurai's creed, to be willing to die at any moment, was dramatically spelled out by the *Hagakure*.[34] According to the *Hagakure*, the important concern was not whether one lived or died, but whether one was pure, simple, single-minded, took full responsibility for doing one's duty, and unconditionally served one's master without concern for self.

Although seppuku may seem like a violent death to the observer, it was designed to enable the samurai to die with the greatest peace and dignity. It is particularly noteworthy that the samurai's code of suicide included a provision for euthanasia: the *kaishakunin* (attendant). Cutting of the *hara* (belly) alone was very painful, but would not lead to a swift death. After cutting their hara, few samurai had enough strength to cut their own necks or spines. Yet without cutting their necks, the pain of the opened hara would continue for minutes or even hours prior to death. Therefore, the samurai would prearrange with one or more kaishakunin to assist his suicide.

While the samurai steadied his mind and prepared to die in peace, the kaishakunin would wait by his side. If the samurai spoke to the kaishakunin before or during the seppuku ceremony, the standard response was *go anshin* (set your mind at peace). All of the interactions and conversations surrounding an officially ordered seppuku were also fixed by tradition, so that the suicide might die with the least tension and greatest peace of mind. After the samurai had finished cutting to the prearranged point or had given some other signal, it was the duty of the kaishakunin to cut the neck of the samurai, to terminate his pain by administering the coup de grace.[35]

Many samurai suicides were in fact the moral equivalent of euthanasia. The reasons for a samurai's suicide were either to avoid an inevitable death at the hands of others or to escape a longer period of unbearable pain or psychological misery while unable to be an active fruitful member of society. These are exactly the sorts of situations in which euthanasia is desired today: to avoid an inevitable death at the hands of others (including disease), or to escape a longer period of pain or misery while unable to be a fruitful, active member of society.

Most Japanese are now cut down in their seventies by cancer and other diseases, rather than in their youth on a battlefield. Regardless of whether the person is hopelessly surrounded by enemies on a battlefield or hopelessly defeated by enemy organisms within his body, the morality of the situation is logically the same. It might be argued that there is a difference between the pain or misery of the permanent incapacitation of a samurai, and the pain or misery of the permanent incapacitation of hospital patients. But if anything, hospital patients are in even less of a position to contribute to society or feel valued than were the samurai, so they have even more reason to be granted the option of leaving this world when they choose.

The samurai tradition shows that the important issue is not the level of physical pain, but the prospect for meaningful and productive interaction with other members of society. If there are no prospects for such interactions, then samurai society claimed no right to prevent the person from seeking more meaningful experiences in another world.

Now in both cases, there may be relatives or retainers in the area who do not wish to see someone die. The issue in these cases is not whether the besieged person will die or not, it is only a questionof how soon and in what manner. From ancient times, Japanese have respected the right of the individual to choose that moment and manner of dying. This Buddhist principle ought to apply equally well to the modern medical battles against the enemies of the body. The argument that if a body still has a face it is still a person to those around him is a basically un-Buddhist failure to understand the difference between body and life, the importance of each person's determination of his or her own mental states, and the importance of placing mercy over desire in Buddhism.

Of course there need to be safeguards in such situations, and those safeguards have already been spelled out by the decision of the Nagoya High Court. In a case of euthanasia, the Nagoya High Court (22 December 1962) defined certain conditions under which euthanasia could be considered acceptable:

1. The disease is considered terminal and incurable with present medical knowledge.
2. The pain is unbearable, both for the patient and those around him.
3. The death is for the purpose of peaceful passing.
4. The person himself has requested the death while conscious and sane.

5. The killing is done by a doctor.
6. The method of killing is humane.

If these safeguards are followed, it seems there is no moral reason that Buddhists should oppose euthanasia. Practically speaking, however, as we noted earlier, it is difficult to determine whether a Japanese doctor has abided by all of these criteria. Some legal safeguards and checks and balances on the abuses of medical power need to be built into the Japanese hospital system before euthanasia along the above guidelines will really prove safe and free from danger of abuse.

Rights and Responsibilities

There are Japanese who hold that the Japanese lack the independent decision-making abilities of Western people, and that therefore doctors should make the decisions for their patients. This logic is backwards. The reason patients cannot make good independent judgments is because the doctors refuse them the information and freedom to do so, not because they lack the mental or personal abilities to make judgments.[36] Buddhism has always recognized the importance of individual choice despite social pressures; examples range from the Buddha himself, through Kūkai, Hōnen, Shinran, and Nagamatsu Nissen. The abilities of the Japanese to take personal responsibility for important decisions in times of stress, danger, or anguish has been repeatedly shown in the historical examples of these bold Buddhist reformers.

In order for patients to make intelligent decisions about when and how they want to die, they need to know the facts about the nature of their diseases: not only the real names, but the realistic prospects and alternative outcomes of all available forms of treatment. This means renouncing the paternalistic model held by present Japanese medicine and granting substantial freedom to patients in deciding their own cases. Some Japanese doctors have argued that patients don't really want to know the bad news about themselves, that knowing the truth may harm their conditions, and that the physician can judge more intelligently than the patient. However, studies in the West show that none of these claims is true. As Bok points out, "the attitude that what [the patient] doesn't know won't hurt him is proving unrealistic—it is rather what patients do not know but vaguely suspect that causes them corrosive worry."[37]

People recover faster from surgery and tolerate pain with less medication when they understand their own medical problems and what can and cannot be done about them.[38] There is no reason to believe that these findings, long known in Western medicine, should prove any different for Japanese Buddhists. In any case, doctors' withholding of information from patients is not based on statistical proof or ethical principles, but based on the physicians' desires to retain control over patients.[39] This is a situation which clear-thinking Buddhists naturally oppose.

One important question for Buddhists remains: What, if any, are the differences between suicide and euthanasia? Obviously one important difference is in the case where the person receiving euthanasia is unconscious. In this case, we have no way of knowing whether the patient genuinely desires euthanasia unless he or she has previously made a declaration of wishes in a living will. On the other hand, once the consciousness has permanently dissociated itself from the body, there is no Buddhist reason to continue to nourish or stimulate the body, for the body deprived of its khandhās is not a person. The Japan Society for Dying with Dignity (*Songenshi Kyōkai*) has done much to improve the ability of individual Japanese to choose the time and manner of their deaths.

Another issue is the relation of pain killing to prolonging life and hastening death itself. The Japan Songenshi Kyōkai proposes administering of painkilling drugs even if they hasten the death of the patient. Buddhists agree that relief of pain is compassionate, and whether death is hastened or not is not the primary issue. However, consider a case where the pain is extreme and only very strong drugs will stop the pain. Here there may be only a choice between no treatment at all, pain killing which only blurs or confuses the mind of the patient, and treatment which hastens the end while keeping the mind clear.

In such a situation, Buddhists would first prefer the most natural way of no treatment at all. But if they were unable to focus their minds or be at peace because of the great pain, Buddhists would choose the last option, because clarity of consciousness at the moment of death is so important in Buddhism.

Doctors who do not like the idea of shortening a person's life might prefer to prolong the material life processes, regardless of the mental quality of that life. This is where Buddhists disagree with materialistic Western medicine. But there need be no conflict between Buddhism and medicine. Following guidelines such as those of the Nagoya court, patients potentially eligible for euthanasia are going to die soon anyway, so that is not the fault of the doctor. There is no reason to assign the doctor the responsibility for the death of the patient. And patients have the right to determine the time of their own death. The fact that they are too weak to hold swords or cut short their own lives with their own hands is not morally significant. The one who understands and compassionately assists those whose minds are clear, calm, and ready for death, then, is also following Buddhist morality.

In summary, the important issue for Buddhists here is whether or not individuals will be allowed responsibility for their own lives and fates. The entire Buddhist tradition, particularly within Japan, argues that personal choice in the manner of death is of paramount importance, and anything done by others to dim the mind or deprive the dying person of such choice is a violation of Buddhist principles. Japanese Buddhists may respect this decision more than Western cultures, and thus lead humanitarian bioethics toward a different perspective on dignified death.

NOTES

BIBLIOGRAPHY

INDEX

Notes

1. Rebirth in Early Buddhism

1. Roy Amore traces this practice back to the *Visuddhimagga*; see Roy Amore, "The Heterodox Philosophical Systems," in *Death and Eastern Thought*, ed. Frederick H. Holck (Nashville: Abingdon Press, 1974), 134.

2. Lynn A. DeSilva, *The Problem of the Self in Buddhism and Christianity* (Colombo, Sri Lanka: Study Centre for Religion and Society, 1975), 20.

3. S. Radhakrishnan, *Eastern Religions and Western Thought* (London: Oxford University Press, 1939), 83.

4. *Milindapanha*, quoted in Theodore deBary, ed., *The Buddhist Tradition* (New York: Modern Library, 1969), 30–32.

5. See DeSilva, *Problem of the Self*, 28.

6. *Mahāvagga*, trans. Narada-Thera, in *The Buddha and His Teachings* (Colombo, Sri Lanka: Vajiraramaya, 1964), 100–102.

7. K. N. Jayatilleke, *The Message of the Buddha* (New York: The Free Press, 1974), 134.

8. K. N. Upadhyaya, *Early Buddhism and the Bhagavad Gita* (Delhi: Motilal Banarsidas, 1971), 368.

9. Mahāvagga, 6.21.1–10, *Vinaya Pitaka*; see also Atthaka-Nipata, 12.4, *Anguttara Nikāya*.

10. J. G. Jennings, *The Vedantic Buddhism of the Buddha* (Delhi: Motilal Banarsidas, 1947), xxxvii.

11. *Milindapanha*, ed. V. Trenckner (London: Luzac, 1962), 46–48.

12. Jayatilleke, *Message*, 119.

13. Govind Chandra Pande, *Studies in the Origins of Buddhism* (Delhi: Motilal Banarsidas, 1957), 493–95.

14. Upadhyaya, *Early Buddhism*, 373–76.

15. Pande, *Studies*, 490 n. 223.

16. E. R. Sarathchandra, *The Buddhist Psychology of Perception* (Colombo, Sri Lanka: Ceylon University Press, 1958), 80–82.

17. See Alex Wayman, "The Intermediate State Dispute," in *Buddhist Studies in Honour of I. B. Horner*, ed. L. Cousins, A. Kunst, and K. R. Norman (Dordrecht: D. Reidel, 1974), 238 nn. 30, 34.

18. Upadhyaya, *Early Buddhism*, 302–4.

19. *Mahākamma*, in Hendrik Kern, *Histoire du Bouddhisme dans l'Inde*, trans. Gédéon Huet (Paris: E. Leroux, 1901), 1:260–62.

20. Mahāthera Nyanatiloka, *Karma and Rebirth* (Colombo, Sri Lanka: Buddhist Publication Society, 1955), 2.

21. See also the numerous scriptural references adduced by Francis Story, *Rebirth as Doctrine and Experience* (Kandy: Buddhist Publication Society, 1975), 65–67.

22. See Amore, "Philosophical Systems," 124.

23. See Jayatilleke, *Message*, 135, 143.

24. See Bimala Churn Law, *Heaven and Hell in Buddhist Perspective* (Varanasi: Bhartiya Publishers, 1973) and *The Buddhist Conception of Spirits* (Varanasi: Bhartiya Publishers, 1974).

2. The Nirvana Alternative

1. Jennings, *Vedantic Buddhism*, xliii.

2. See Upadhyaya, *Early Buddhism*, 337, 341.

3. Eugene Burnouf, *Introduction à l'histoire du bouddhisme indien* (Paris: Maisonneuve et Cie, 1876), 525.

4. Barthelemy Saint-Hilaire, *The Buddha and His Religion*, 3d ed., trans. L. Ensor (London: George Routledge, 1895), v–vi.

5. Max Müller, *Selected Essays on Language, Mythology, and Religion* (London: Longman's, Green & Co., 1881) 2:301–3.

6. "Nirvana," in *A Dictionary of the Pali Language*, ed. Robert Caesar Childers (London: Kegan Paul, Trench, Trubner, and Co., 1872–1875), 266b.

7. James D'Alwis, *Buddhist Nirvāna: A Review of Max Müller's Dhammapāda* (Colombo, Sri Lanka: William Skeen, 1871), 40–43.

8. F. T. Stcherbatsky, *Buddhist Logic* (Leningrad: Academy of Sciences of the USSR, 1930–32), 2:868.

9. Stcherbatsky, *Buddhist Logic*, 2:871–72.

10. George Grimm, *The Doctrine of the Buddha*, 2d ed. (Berlin: Akademie-Verlag, 1958), 5.

11. *Digha Nikāya*, 1.200, quoted in Jayatilleke, *Message*, 200.

12. Burnouf, *Introduction*, 525.

13. Max Müller, *Selected Essays*, 2:306.

14. C. A. F. Rhys-Davids, "A Historical Aspect of Nirvana," in *Wayfarer's Words* (London: Luzac and Co., 1941), 2:657.

15. E. J. Thomas, *The History of Buddhist Thought*, 2d ed. (London: Routledge and Kegan Paul, 1948), 127–30.

16. Heinrich Dumoulin, *History of Zen Buddhism*, trans. Paul Peachey (New York: Pantheon Books, 1963), 292 n. 21.

17. Louis de LaVallée Poussin, *Bouddhisme: Opinions sur l'histoire de la dogmatique* (Paris: Gabriel Beauchesne et Cie., 1908), 75.

18. Louis de LaVallée Poussin, *Le Dogme et la philosophie du bouddhisme* (Paris: Gabriel Beauchesne, 1930), 51.

19. Jean Baptiste François Obry, *Du Nirvāna bouddhique en reponse à M. Barthelemy Saint-Hilaire* (Paris: Auguste Durand, 1863), 85.

20. Philippe Edouard Foucaux, *Doctrine des bouddhistes sur le nirvāna* (Paris: Benjamin Duprat, 1864), 13–16.

21. F. Otto Schrader, "On the Problem of Nirvana," *Journal of the Pali Text Society* (unnumbered volume, 1904–5): 165.

22. Norman Pliny Jacobson, *Buddhism, The Religion of Analysis* (New York: Humanities Press, 1965), 147.

23. T. Magness quotes Ven. Chao Khun Monghol Thepmuni, in *Samma Samadhi* (Thonburi, Thailand: Bhasicharoen, 1955), 17–18.

24. T. R. V. Murti, *The Central Philosophy of Buddhism* (London: George Allen and Unwin, 1955), 48.

25. Frauwallner and Hoppe are quoted in the preface to Grimm, *The Doctrine of the Buddha*, 3–5.

26. Upadhyaya, *Early Buddhism*, 342.

27. DeSilva, *Problem of the Self*, 37–39.

28. Henry T. Colebrooke, *Miscellaneous Essays*, ed. E. B. Cowell (London: Trubner and Co., 1873), 2:425.

29. "Nirvāna," in *The Pali Text Society's Pali-English Dictionary*, ed. T. W. Rhys-Davids and W. Stede (London: Luzac and Co., 1921–25), 326a.

30. Amore, "Philosophical Systems," 128 and quoting the *Samyutta Nikāya* 3.251.

31. Amore, "Philosophical Systems," 129, 161 nn. 20–22.

32. David J. Kalupahana, *Buddhist Philosophy: A Historical Analysis* (Honolulu: University Press of Hawaii, 1976), 87.

33. David J. Kalupahana, *Causality: The Central Philosophy of Buddhism* (Honolulu: University Press of Hawaii, 1975), 180.

34. Sōgen Yamakami, *Systems of Buddhistic Thought* (Calcutta: University of Calcutta Press, 1912), 33.

35. D. T. Suzuki, *Outlines of Mahāyāna Buddhism* (New York: Schocken Books, 1963), 51.

36. *Milindapanha*, 73. In his introduction to this passage, deBary concludes that nirvana "is not total annihilation, but at the same time it involves the complete dis-integration of the phenomenal personality—a paradox which cannot be explained in words" (*The Buddhist Tradition*, 30).

37. Pande, *Studies*, 509.

38. P. Lakshmi Narasu, *The Essence of Buddhism* (Bombay: Thacker and Co., 1907), 224–25.

39. Edward Conze, *Buddhism: Its Essence and Development* (Oxford: Bruno Cassirer, 1951), 110.

40. Sarathchandra, *Buddhist Psychology*, 103.

41. *Udāna*, in Vol. 8 of *Minor Anthologies of the Pali Canon*, trans. F. L. Woodward (London: Oxford University Press, 1948), 2.98.

42. See Pande, *Studies*, 510.

43. Jayatilleke, *Message*, 122.

44. See Upadhyaya, *Early Buddhism*, 343.

45. Quoted in Upadhyaya, *Early Buddhism*, 343.

3. The Afterlife in Pure Land Buddhism

1. *Anguttara Nikāya* [Gradual Sayings], 1.167. Unless otherwise specified, references are to editions of the Pali Text Society, ed. Thomas or C. A. F. Rhys-Davids (London: Oxford University Press).

2. *Kuddhakapātha*, 8.13–16. See also James P. McDermott, "Nibbana as a Reward for Kamma," *Journal of the American Oriental Society* 93.3 (1973): 344–47.

3. *Kathāvatthu*, 7.6. See also James P. McDermott, "The *Kathāvatthu* Kamma Debates," *Journal of the American Oriental Society* 95.3 (1975): 430.

4. *Milindapanha*, 294–97. See also James P. McDermott, "Kamma in the *Milindapanha*," *Journal of the American Oriental Society* 97.4 (1977): 463.

5. See Whalen Lai, "Tales of Rebirths and the Later Pure Land Tradition in China," in *Berkeley Buddhist Studies*, 3, ed. Michael Solomon. Forthcoming.

6. Karl L. Reichelt, *Truth and Tradition in Chinese Buddhism*, trans. K. V. Bugge (1928; reprint, New York: Paragon Book Reprints, 1968), 92, 115.

7. J. J. M. deGroot, *The Religious System of China* (Taipei: Cheng Wen Publishers, 1972), 4:96, 113, 421–22.

8. Teresina Rowell, "The Background and Early Use of the *Buddhaksetra* Concept," *Eastern Buddhist* 6 (1934): 202, 426; 7 (1937): 131–69.

9. *Dīgha Nikāya*, 3.146–56; *Samyutta Nikāya*, 1.227, 293.

10. Rowell, "Background and Early Use," 419–24.

11. *Dīgha Nikāya*, 2.25; *Anguttara Nikāya*, 1.10, 26–27.

12. Rowell, "Background and Early Use," 219, 415.

13. Kōtatsu Fujita, *Genshi Jōdō Shisō no Kenkyū* (Tokyo: Iwanami Shoten, 1970), 487–90.

14. Fujita, *Genshi Jōdō Shisō*, 496; See also 499 n.16.

15. Gregory Schopen, "Sukhāvati as a Generalized Religious Goal in Sanskrit Mahāyāna Sūtra Literature," *Indo-Iranian Journal* 19 (Aug.–Sept. 1977): 177–80, 204–5.

16. Erik Zürcher, *The Buddhist Conquest of China* (Leiden: Brill, 1959), 221.

17. Fujita, *Genshi Jōdō Shisō*, 51–61, 116–20.

18. *Taishō Shinshū Daizōkyō*, ed. Junjirō Takayanagi et al. (Tokyo: Taishō Shinshū Daizōkyō Kankōkai, 1962), 26.230–33. This is the standard reference for sutras in the Sino-Japanese tradition; hereafter abbreviated *Taishō*.

19. Daigan Matsunaga, trans., *The Foundation of Japanese Buddhism* (Tokyo: Buddhist Books International, 1976), 2:22–23, 30.

20. These texts are found in Max Müller, ed., *Sacred Books of the East* (Oxford: Clarendon Press, 1894), 49:34–40; 93–95. For a comparative catalog of the contents of the sutras, see Fujita, *Genshi Jōdō Shisō*, 448–50.

21. Müller, *Sacred Books*, 52.

22. Müller, *Sacred Books*, 38.

23. Müller, *Sacred Books*, 42–44.

24. See *Taishō*, 26.230–33; Hsuan Hua, *A General Explanation of the Buddha Speaks of Amitabha Sutra* (San Francisco: Buddhist Text Translation Society, 1974), 117.

25. Müller, *Sacred Books*, 62–66.

26. T'an-luan, "A Short Essay on the Pure Land," trans. Leo Pruden, *Eastern Buddhist*, n.s., 7.1 (May 1975): 87.

27. See Suzuki's "Appendices" to Shinran, in D. T. Suzuki, trans., *Kyōgyōshinshō* (Kyoto: Shinshū Ōtaniha, 1973), 350–440. For further discussions of the *Trikāya*, see D. T. Suzuki, *Studies in the Lankāvatāra Sūtra* (London: Routledge and Kegan Paul, 1930), esp. 308–13 and Gadjin Nagao, "On the Theory of the Buddha Body," *Eastern Buddhist*, n.s., 4.1 (May 1973): 36.

28. Julian Pas, "Dimensions in the Life and Thought of Shan-tao" (Paper delivered at the Society for the Study of Chinese Religion, St. Louis, Oct. 1976), 14.

29. David Chappell, "Chinese Buddhist Interpretations of the Pure Lands," in *Buddhist and Taoist Studies*, 1, ed. David Chappell and Michael Saso (Honolulu: University Press of Hawaii, 1977), 30–32, shows how Chih-i and Hui-yuan reduced the Pure Land into simply a higher level of samsara or illusion.

30. *Taishō*, 26:230–33; an unpublished translation by Kenjō Urakami of this text is entitled "Gatha Discourse on the Sutra of the Buddha of Infinite Life," 7.

31. Roger Corless, "T'an-luan's Commentary on the Pure Land Discourse" (Ph.D. diss., University of Wisconsin, 1973), 140–41.

32. Ryōsetsu Fujiwara, *The Way to Nirvāna* (Tokyo: Kyōiku Shin-chōsha, 1974), 54–56. See also T'an-luan, "Short Essay," 82.

33. Chappell, "Chinese Buddhist Interpretations," 37–39.

34. Chappell, "Chinese Buddhist Interpretations," 42–46.

35. Rowell, "Background and Early Use," 228.

36. Rowell, "Background and Early Use," 397.

37. *Eastern Buddhist* 1.2 (1921): 152 gives a translation of the *Avatamsaka Sutra*, presumably translated by D. T. Suzuki.

4. Finding the Pure Land Oneself

1. Julian Pas, "Shan-tao's Interpretations of the Meditative Vision of Amitāyus," *History of Religions* 14.2 (1974): 100–103.
2. *Meditation on Amitayus [Amitāyur-dhyāna-sūtra]*, trans. Junjiro Takakusu, in Müller, ed. *Sacred Books*, 186; above descriptions excerpted from 170–80.
3. Pas, "Dimensions," 22, 25.
4. Pas, "Interpretations," 105.
5. Allan Andrews, *The Teachings Essential for Rebirth, A Study of Genshin's Ōjōyōshū* (Tokyo: Sophia University, 1974), 78.
6. Zürcher, *Buddhist Conquest*, 219–20.
7. Kenneth K. S. Ch'en, *Buddhism in China* (Princeton: Princeton University Press, 1964), 111.
8. Zürcher, *Buddhist Conquest*, 221; this means he saw the Pure Land at death.
9. Zürcher, *Buddhist Conquest*, 227–28.
10. Zenryū Tsukamoto, *Bukkyō no Shisō, Chūgoku Jōdō* (Tokyo: Kadokawa Shoten, 1968), 8:283.
11. Pas, "Interpretations," 113–15; "Dimensions," 10.
12. David Chappell, "The Formation of the Pure Land Movement in China: Tao-ch'o and Shan-tao," in *Berkeley Buddhist Studies*, 3, ed. Michael Solomon. Forthcoming. Tsukamoto believes that Shan-tao himself may have suicided (273, 288).
13. Fujiwara, *Way to Nirvāna*, 134–36; 146. See also H. H. Coates and Ryūgaku Ishizuka, *Hōnen The Buddhist Saint* (Kyoto: Chionin, 1925), 574.
14. Chih-pan, *A Chronicle of Buddhism in China, 581–960 A.D.*, ed. and trans. Jan Yun Hua (Santiniketan: Visvabharati, 1966), 69–73.
15. M. W. deVisser, *Ancient Buddhism in Japan* (Leiden: E. J. Brill, 1935), 334, 327.
16. Coates and Ishizuka, *Hōnen*, 493. Rensei himself predicted the hour of his death based on visions, and his passing was accompanied by music, 499.

17. Matsunaga, *Foundation*, 13–14.

18. Matsunaga, *Foundation*, 13–14.

19. Coates and Ishizuka, *Hōnen*, 203.

20. Shōjun Bandō, "Myōe's Criticisms of Hōnen's Doctrine," *Eastern Buddhist*, n.s., 7.1 (May 1974): 41–42.

21. "Zammai Hōtoki" in *Hōnen Shōnin den Zenshū* (Osaka: Hōnen Shōnin den Zenshū Kankōkai, 1967), 863–64.

22. Jikai Fujikoshi, "Bannen no Hōnen Shōnin," *Indogaku Bukkyōgaku Kenkyū* 20.1 (Dec. 1971): 121–27. See also Enchō Tamura, *Hōnen Shōnin den no Kenkyū* (Kyoto: Hōzōkan, 1972), Appendix 24–38.

23. See George Tanabe, "Myōe Shōnin: Tradition and Reform in Early Kamakura Buddhism" (Ph.D. diss., Columbia University, 1983), 174–78.

24. Bandō, "Myōe's Criticisms," 40.

25. Myōe, "Zaijarin," in *Kamakura Kyū Bukkyō*, ed. Shigeo Kamata and Tanaka Hisao, in *Nihon Shisō Taikei* (Tokyo: Iwanami Shoten, 1971), 15:317b–318; cf. 367a.

26. Fujita, *Genshi Jōdo Shisō*, 575.

27. *Milindapanha*, 80, 17–27.

28. Fujita, *Genshi Jōdo Shisō*, 577, 580 n.12.

29. Müller's translation, in Müller, *Sacred Books*, 15.

30. Müller's translation, in Müller, *Sacred Books*, 99.

31. J. Takakusu's translation in Müller, *Sacred Books*, 189–98.

32. Shan-tao is quoted by Genshin's *Ōjōyōshū*; as translated by Andrews, *Teachings*, 83.

33. See "Hōnen's Teachings to Lay and Clerical Disciples" in Coates and Ishizuka, *Hōnen*. The notion of constant recitation is also predicated upon the fact that we must be prepared to die at any moment, 440–41.

34. *Meditation on Amitāyus* [*Amitāyur-dhyāna-sūtra*], trans. J. Takakusu, in Müller, *Sacred Books*, 186.

35. T'an-luan, "Short Essay," 83.

36. Coates and Ishizuka, *Hōnen*, 57.

37. deGroot, *Religious System of China*, 96, 113, 421–22.

38. deVisser, *Ancient Buddhism*, 328.

39. Zürcher, *Buddhist Conquest*, 222.

40. Zürcher, *Buddhist Conquest*, 399.

41. Ch'en, *Buddhism in China*, 344.

42. Lai, "Tales of Rebirths," 16.

43. Chappell, "Formation," 26.

44. On Chia-ts'ai, see Senshū Ogasawara, *Chūgoku Jōdōkyō no Kenkyū* (Kyoto: Heirakuji, 1951), 81–89, 107–8.

45. Accounts from the *Ching-t'u lun* found in *Taishō*, 47.97–98.

46. *Taishō*, 47.99.

47. See also Ogasawara, *Chūgoku Jōdōkyō*, 106–10.

48. Lai, "Tales of Rebirths," 26.

49. Kyōko Nakamura, *Miraculous Stories from the Japanese Buddhist Tradition* [The *Ryōiki*] (Cambridge: Harvard University Press, 1973), esp. 50, 122. All further citations are from this collection.

50. D. E. Mills, *A Collection of Tales from Uji* (Cambridge: Cambridge University Press, 1970).

51. See Akehisa Shigematsu, "Ōjōden no Kenkyū," *Nagoya Daigaku Bungakubu Kenkyū Ronsho, Shigakuhen* 8 (1960): 23, 48–52.

52. M. W. deVisser, *The Bodhisattva Ti-tsang [Jizō] in China and Japan* (Berlin: Oesterheld and Co., 1914), 51–53.

53. Carmen Blacker, "Other World Journeys in Japan," in *The Journey to the Other World*, ed. H. R. E. Davidson (Cambridge: D. S. Brewer, 1975), 45.

54. Coates and Ishizuka, *Hōnen*, 634.

55. Matsunaga, *Foundation*, 58.

56. Mills, *Tales from Uji*, 91.

57. deVisser, *Bodhisattva*, 88–89.

58. Lai, "Tales of Rebirths," 45.

59. Here Chu-hung anticipates modern scholars' arguments by four centuries. See Senshū Ogasawara, *Chūgoku Kinsei Jōdōkyōshi no Kenkyū* (Kyoto: Hyakka-en, 1963), 217.

60. Fujita, *Genshi Jōdō Shisō*, 546–47.

61. Fujiwara, *Way to Nirvāna*, 58; T'an-luan, "Short Essay," 95.

62. Chappell, "Formation," 17–20.

63. Pas, "Dimensions," 11, 25.

64. deVisser, *Ancient Buddhism*, 327, 334.

65. Cf. Kaoru Inoue, *Gyōki* (Tokyo: Yoshikawa Kobunkan, 1958), and Ichirō Hori, *Kūya* (Tokyo: Yoshikawa Kobunkan, 1958).

66. "Senchakushū," in *Hōnen Shōnin den Zenshū* (Osaka: Hōnen Shōnin den Zenshū Kankōkai, 1967), 350; cf. "Senchakushū Mitsuyō-

ketsu," in *Jōdōshū Zensho* (Tokyo: Jōdōshū Shūten Kankōkai, 1910), 8.247a.

67. Alfred Bloom, *Shinran's Gospel of Pure Grace* (Tucson: University of Arizona, 1965), esp. 73–74.

68. Kimura cites a letter in which Shinran says he looks forward to meeting one of his dying disciples in person again after death. See Kiyotaka Kimura, *Shoki Chūgoku Kegon Shisō no Kenkyū* (Tokyo: Shunjū-sha, 1977).

69. E.g., his passages in *Tannisho*, quoted in deBary, 339–40.

70. Yoshifumi Ueda, ed. and trans., *Notes on the Essentials of Faith Alone* [Shinran's *Yuishinsho-mon'i*] (Kyoto: Hongwanji International Center, 1979), 33–34, 39, 42.

71. D. T. Suzuki, *A Miscellany on the Shin Teaching of Buddhism* (Kyoto: Shinshū Ōtaniha Shomusho, 1949), 139, 148.

72. See the "demythologizing" efforts throughout Gembō Hoshino, *Shinshū no Tetsugakuteki Rikai* (Kyoto: Hōzōkan, 1972).

73. See for example Karlis Osis and Erlendur Haraldsson, *At the Hour of Death* (New York: Avon, 1977) and Kenneth Ring, *Life at Death* (New York: Coward, McCann and Geoghegan, 1980).

74. Maitland Baldwin, "Hallucinations in Neurologic Syndromes," in *Hallucinations*, ed. L. J. West (New York: Grune and Stratton, 1962), 78–81.

75. A. J. Silverman et al., "Hallucinations in Sensory Deprivation," in *Hallucinations*, ed. L. J. West (New York: Grune and Stratton, 1962), 156–58.

76. Osis and Haraldsson, *At the Hour of Death*, 156, 172.

77. Wellesley T. Pole, *Private Dowding* (London: J. M. Watkins, 1917), 101.

78. Junjirō Takakusu, *Essentials of Buddhist Philosophy* (Honolulu: University Press of Hawaii, 1947), 166. See also August K. Reischauer, *Studies in Japanese Buddhism* (New York: Macmillan Co., 1917), 69.

79. H. H. Price, "Survival and the Idea of Another World," *Proceedings of the Society of Psychical Research* 50.182 (Jan. 1953): 23–25.

5. Tibetan Buddhism and the Book of the Dead

1. Giuseppe Tucci, *Tibet, Land of Snows*, trans. J. E. S. Driver (New York: Stein and Day, 1967), 19–24.

2. Helmut Hoffman, *The Religions of Tibet* (London: George Allen and Unwin, 1961), 17–23.

3. Robert K. Ekvall, *Religious Observances in Tibet* (Chicago: University of Chicago Press, 1964), 39.

4. Helmut Hoffman et al., *Tibet: A Handbook* (Bloomington: Indiana University Research Center for the Language Sciences, 1975), 94–100, 162.

5. Rene de Nebesky-Wojkowitz, *Oracles and Demons of Tibet* (The Hague: Mouton, 1956), 414–40.

6. Tucci, *Tibet*, 165.

7. Laurence Austine Waddell, *The Buddhism of Tibet, or Lamaism* (Cambridge: W. Heffer and Sons, 1934), 562.

8. Waddell, *Buddhism of Tibet*, 128.

9. Hoffman, *Religions*, 167.

10. Waddell, *Buddhism of Tibet*, 217, 493.

11. J. E. Ellam, *The Religion of Tibet* (New York: E. P. Dutton, 1927), 34–36.

12. Hoffman, *Handbook*, 115–25.

13. Tucci, *Tibet*, 73–78.

14. W. Y. Evans-Wentz, *Tibetan Yoga and Secret Doctrines* (London: Oxford University Press, 1935), 232–33.

15. Evans-Wentz, *Tibetan Yoga*, 237–38, 254.

16. See Waddell, *Buddhism of Tibet*, 10–77; Tucci, *Tibet*, 24–60.

17. Hoffman, *Religions*, 63–64.

18. Hoffman, *Handbook*, 162.

19. Hoffman, *Religions*, 64.

20. Anagarika Govinda, *Foundations of Tibetan Mysticism* (New York: E. P. Dutton, 1960), 122–23.

21. Waddell, *Buddhism of Tibet*, 789–93.

22. Evans-Wentz, *Tibetan Yoga*, 234–43.

23. Jeffrey Hopkins and Lati Rinpochay, *Death, Intermediate State, and Rebirth in Tibetan Buddhism* (Ithaca, N.Y.: Snow Lion Publications, 1979), 15–20.

24. Waddell, *Buddhism of Tibet*, 488–89.

25. Evans-Wentz, *Tibetan Yoga*, 170.

26. Hoffman, *Handbook*, 153.

27. Evans-Wentz, *Tibetan Yoga*, 232.

28. John Woodroffe, "The Science Of Death," Foreword to *[The*

Tibetan] Book of the Dead, ed. W. Y. Evans-Wentz, trans. Kazi Dawa-Samdup (London: Oxford University Press, 1957), lxxi.

29. Woodroffe, "Science Of Death," lxxii–lxxiv.

30. Evans-Wentz, *Tibetan Yoga*, 236; *[The Tibetan] Book of the Dead*, ed. W. Y. Evans-Wentz, trans. Kazi Dawa-Samdup (London: Oxford University Press, 1957), 91.

31. Woodroffe, "Science Of Death," lxxiv.

32. Govinda, *Foundations*, 249–52.

33. Tucci, *Tibet*, 89.

34. *Book of the Dead*, 160–66.

35. Hoffman, *Handbook*, 162–63.

36. *Book of the Dead*, 180–85.

37. Evans-Wentz, *Tibetan Yoga*, 246.

38. Hoffman, *Handbook*, 167.

39. Ellam, *Religion of Tibet*, 42–43.

40. Waddell, *Buddhism of Tibet*, 229–53.

41. A. David-Neel, *Mystiques et magiciens du Thibet* (Paris: Plon, 1930), 122–26.

42. Waddell, *Buddhism of Tibet*, 494.

43. Govinda, *Foundations*, 125.

44. Woodroffe, "Science Of Death," lxxv.

45. Evans-Wentz, *Tibetan Yoga*, 167.

46. W. Y. Evans-Wentz, Introduction to *[The Tibetan] Book of the Dead*, ed. W. Y. Evans-Wentz, trans. Kazi Dawa-Samdup (London: Oxford University Press, 1957), xxxiv.

6. Models for Survival

1. Ring, *Life at Death*, 23–33.

2. Robert Kastenbaum, *Between Life and Death* (New York: Springer-Verlag, 1979), esp. 16, 20, 22. Kastenbaum argues against any presentation that might imply death is "fun" or could provide an easy release from suffering.

3. Kastenbaum, *Between Life and Death*, 180.

4. John Hick, *Death and Eternal Life* (New York: Harper and Row, 1976), 414–16.

5. Yogi Ramacharaka, *The Life Beyond Death* (Chicago: Yogi Publication Society, 1940), 80.

6. Nils O. Jacobson, *Life Without Death?*, trans. Sheila La Farge (New York: Delacorte Press, 1974), 266.

7. Maurice Rawlings' *Beyond Death's Door* (Nashville: Thomas Nelson, 1978) shows that even good Christians occasionally undergo "hellish" near-death experiences.

8. This thesis is developed by Michael Grosso, "Possible Nature of Post-Mortem States," *Journal of the American Society for Psychical Research* 74.4 (1980): 422.

9. Ian Stevenson, *Children Who Remember Previous Lives* (Charlottesville: University Press of Virginia, 1987); the bibliography to this volume attests to Stevenson's exhaustive research on this subject.

10. Hick, *Death and Eternal Life*, 392, 457.

11. This seems true even of Europeans dying in Asia. See Ian Stevenson, "Carington's Psychon Theory as Applied to Cases of the Reincarnation Type," *Journal of the American Society for Psychical Research* 67.2 (1973): 132.

12. Stevenson, "Carington's Psychon Theory," 133, 135.

13. Adrian Parker, *States of Mind* (New York: Taplinger, 1975), 168.

14. Nils O. Jacobson, *Life Without Death?*, 368–69.

15. I have already cited the years elapsing between death and birth in the previous section.

16. J. M. O. Wheatley, "Reincarnation, etc.," in *Philosophical Dimensions of Parapsychology*, ed. Hoyt L. Edge and J. M. O. Wheatley (Springfield, Ill.: Charles C. Thomas, 1976), 118.

17. Wheatley, "Reincarnation, etc.," 111.

18. J. B. Rhine, "Research on Spirit Survival Reexamined," *Journal of Parapsychology* 20.2 (June 1956): 127.

19. J. B. Rhine, "The Science of Nonphysical Nature," in *Philosophy and Parapsychology*, ed. Jan Ludwig (Buffalo: Prometheus, 1978), 125.

20. Hick, *Death and Eternal Life*, 344.

21. R. Binkley, "Philosophy and the Survival Hypothesis," *Journal of the American Society for Psychical Research* 60.1 (1966): 28.

22. John Beloff, "Parapsychology and Its Neighbors," in *Philosoph-*

ical Dimensions of Parapsychology, ed. Hoyt L. Edge and J. M. O. Wheatley (Springfield, Ill.: Charles C. Thomas, 1976), 383.

23. Immanuel Kant, *Kritik der Reinen Vernunft,* 2d ed. (Leipzig: F. Meiner, 1906), 809.

24. William James, "Human Immortality," in *William James on Psychical Research,* ed. Gardner Murphy and Robert Ballou (New York: Viking Press, 1960), 292.

25. Malcolm M. Moncrieff, *The Clairvoyant Theory of Perception* (London: Faber and Faber, 1951), 7.

26. Jonathan Harrison, "Religion and Psychical Research," in *Philosophy and Psychical Research,* ed. Shivesh C. Thakur (London: George Allen and Unwin, 1976), 111.

27. C. D. Broad, *Ethics and the History of Philosophy* (New York: Humanities Press, 1952), x.

28. H. D. Lewis, *The Self and Immortality* (New York: Seabury Press, 1973), 155, 163.

29. See G. N. M. Tyrell, *Apparitions* (London: Duckworth, 1953), 139–54.

30. We speak here not of the "starry eyed" sort of idealism found in people with *ideals,* but rather of the philosophical idealism that holds that the underlying essence of all things is *idea.*

31. Tyrell, quoted by David Ellis, "The Chemistry of Psi," in *Parapsychology and the Sciences,* ed. Alan Angoff and Betty Shapin (New York: Parapsychology Foundation, 1974), 214.

32. See Beloff, "Parapsychology," 384.

33. Gardner Murphy, "Psychical Research and the Mind-Body Relation," *Journal of the American Society for Psychical Research* 40.2 (1946): 192.

34. Lawrence LeShan, "Physicists and Mystics, Similarities in World-View," *Journal of Transpersonal Psychology* 1.2 (1969): 1–15.

35. Ring, *Life at Death,* 247–48.

36. Ring, *Life at Death,* 296.

37. See Emilio Servadio, "Mind-Body, Reality, and Psi," in *Brain/ Mind and Parapsychology,* ed. Betty Shapin and Lisette Coly (New York: Parapsychology Foundation, 1979), 234–38.

38. Charles C. Tart, "States of Consciousness and the State-Specific Sciences," *Science* 176 (12 June 1972): 1203–10.

39. Non-Western sources emphasize that psychic states are nothing

to explore frivolously or casually; training, discipline, and a master are required to protect a practitioner's sanity.

40. Michael Grosso, "The Survival of Personality in a Mind-Dependent World," *Journal of the American Society for Psychical Research* 73.4 (1979): 369, 376–77.

41. Gardner Murphy, "Field Theory and Survival," *Journal of the American Society for Psychical Research* 39.4 (1945): 200–201.

42. Hick, *Death and Eternal Life*, 464.

43. Grosso, "Survival of Personality," 379.

44. C. J. Ducasse, *A Critical Examination of the Belief in a Life after Death* (Springfield, Ill.: Charles C. Thomas, 1961), 203.

7. Buddhist Ethics of Death and Dying

1. Masahiro Morioka, "Nōshi towa nan deatta ka," *Nihon Rinri Gakkai Kenkyū Happyō Yōshi* [Paper delivered at the Thirty-Ninth Annual Conference of the Japan Ethics Association, Waseda University, Tokyo, 14–15 Oct. 1988], 7.

2. Kazuhiro Anzai, "Nō to sono Ishiki," *Nihon Rinri Gakkai Kenkyū Happyō Yōshi*, 6.

3. Shinjō Kawasaki, "Tōyō Kodai no Seimei Juyō," *Nihon Rinri Gakkai Kenkyū Happyō Yōshi*, 26.

4. Buddhaghosa, *The Visuddhimagga of Buddhaghosacariya* (Cambridge: Harvard University Press, 1950), 299.

5. Kawasaki, "Tōyō Kodai no Seimei Juyō," 27.

6. Tsunesuke Iida, "Bioethicswa nanio nasunoka," *Nihon Rinri Gakkai Kenkyū Happyō Yōshi*, 40–42.

7. Mary Anne Warren, "Do Potential People Have Moral Rights?" *Canadian Journal of Philosophy* 7.2 (1978): 275–89.

8. Carl Becker, "Old and New: Japan's Mechanisms for Crime Control and Social Justice," *Howard Journal of Criminal Justice* 27.4 (Nov. 1988): 284–85.

9. Nobuo Ōhara, "Sei to Shi no Rinrigaku," *Nihon Rinri Gakkai Kenkyū Happyō Yōshi*, 54–55.

10. Carl Becker, "Religion and Politics in Japan," in *Movements and Issues in World Religions*, ed. C. W-H. Fu and G. S. Spiegler (New York: Greenwood Press, 1987), 278.

11. Among the author's students are nurses at such hospitals.

12. Gerald A. Larue, *Euthanasia and Religion: A Survey of the Attitudes of World Religions to the Right-to-Die* (Los Angeles: The Hemlock Society, 1985).

13. See *Hastings Encyclopedia of Religion and Ethics*, ed. James Hastings (New York: Charles Scribner's Sons, 1924), 4.448.

14. *Majjhima Nikāya*, 2.91; 3.258.

15. *Samyutta Nikāya*, trans. C. A. F. Rhys-Davids (London: Pali Text Society, 1930), 5.408.

16. Kōshiro Tamaki, "Shi no Oboegaki," *Bukkyō Shisō* 10 (Sept. 1988): 465–75.

17. cf. *Samyutta Nikāya*, 3.119–24.

18. *Majjhima Nikāya*, 3.263–266 (Channovāda-sutta); *Samyutta Nikāya*, 4.55–60 (Channavaga).

19. *Samyutta Nikāya*, 1.121.

20. *Jātaka Suvarna Prabhāsa*, 206–9.

21. *Acaranga Sūtra*, 1.7.6.

22. A mummified body of one such monk is preserved in the Myōrenji temple, close to Tsukuba University.

23. Senshū Ogasawara, *Chūgoku Jōdōkyō*, 60–63.

24. Thích Nhat-Hanh, *The Lotus in the Sea of Fire* (London: S. C. M. Press, 1967).

25. Isamu Kurita, *Ippen Shōnin, Tabi no Shisakusha* (Tokyo: Shinchōsha, 1977), 165–69.

26. Shunnō Ohashi, *Ippen* (Tokyo: Yoshikawa Kobunkan, 1983), 105–6.

27. *Ippen Goroku*, Scroll 6, Stage 2 [*Maki 6, Dan 2*], reproduced in Makio Takemura et al., *Ippen, Nihonteki naru mono wo megutte* (Tokyo, Shunjūsha, 1991).

28. Kurita, *Ippen Shōnin*, 165–69.

29. Ōhashi, *Ippen*, 107–10.

30. Mori Ōgai, *Takasebune* (Tokyo: Iwanami Bunko, 1978).

31. Jack Seward, *Hara-Kiri: Japanese Ritual Suicide* (Tokyo: Charles E. Tuttle, 1968). Seward describes these and other significant suicides in detail.

32. Monzaemon Chikamatsu, *Major Plays of Chikamatsu*, trans. Donald Keene (New York: Columbia University Press, 1961).

33. Yoshio Fujino, ed., *Kanatehon Chūshingura: Kaishaku to Kenkyū* (Tokyo: Ōfūsha, 1975).

34. Tetsurō Watsuji, ed., *Hagakure* (Tokyo: Iwanami Bunko, 1970).

35. All condensed from Seward, *Hara-Kiri.*

36. Rihito Kimura, "In Japan, Patients Participate but Doctors Decide," *Hastings Center Report* 16.4 (1986): 22–23.

37. See Sisela Bok, *Lying: Moral Choice in Public and Private Life* (New York: Pantheon Books, 1978).

38. Lawrence Egbert et al., "Reduction of Post-operative Pain by Encouragement and Instruction of Patients," *New England Journal of Medicine* 270.16 (1964): 825–27; Howard Waitzskin and John Stoeckle, "The Communication of Information about Illness," *Advances in Psychosomatic Medicine* 8 (1972): 185–215.

39. See Bernard Gert and Charles Culver, "Paternalistic Behavior," *Philosophy and Public Affairs* 6 (Summer 1976): 45–57; Allen Buchanan, "Medical Paternalism," *Philosophy and Public Affairs* 7 (Summer 1978): 370–90.

Bibliography

Akamatsu, Toshihide. *Shinran*. Tokyo: Kobundō, 1961.

Amore, Roy. "The Heterodox Philosophical Systems." In *Death and Eastern Thought*, edited by Frederick H. Holck, 114–60. Nashville: Abingdon Press, 1974.

Andrews, Allan. *The Teachings Essential for Rebirth, A Study of Genshin's Ōjōyōshū*. Tokyo: Sophia University, 1974.

Anguttara Nikāya. In *Sacred Books of the Buddhists*, translated by T. W. Rhys-Davids. London: Oxford University Press, 1899.

Anzai, Kazuhiro. "Nō to sono Ishiki," *Nihon Rinri Gakkai Kenkyū Happyō Yōshi* (Paper delivered at the Thirty-Ninth Annual Conference of the Japan Ethics Association, Waseda University, Tokyo, 14–15 Oct. 1988), 6.

Ashikaga, Atsuji. *Sukhāvatīvyūha*. Kyoto: Hōzōkan, 1965.

Avatamsaka Sūtra. (Translated by D. T. Suzuki) *Eastern Buddhist* 1.2 (1921).

Bacot, Jacques. *Trois mystères tibétains*. Paris: Éditions Bossard, 1921.

———. *La vie de Marpa le "traducteur."* Paris: Librairie Orientaliste, Paul Geunther, 1937.

Baldwin, Maitland. "Hallucinations in Neurologic Syndromes." In *Hallucinations*, edited by L. J. West, 78–81. New York: Grune and Stratton, 1962.

Bandō, Shōjun. "Myōe's Criticisms of Hōnen's Doctrine." *Eastern Buddhist*, n.s. 7.1 (May 1974): 40–44.

Becker, Carl. "Old and New: Japan's Mechanisms for Crime Control

Bibliography

and Social Justice." *Howard Journal of Criminal Justice* 27.4 (Nov. 1988): 283–95.

———. "Religion and Politics in Japan." In *Movements and Issues in World Religions*, edited by C. W-H. Fu and G. S. Spiegler, 277–300. New York: Greenwood Press, 1987.

Bell, Sir Charles. *The People of Tibet.* Oxford: Clarendon Press, 1928.

———. *Portrait of the Dalai Lama.* London: Collins, 1946.

———. *The Religion of Tibet.* Oxford: Clarendon Press, 1931.

Beloff, John. "Parapsychology and Its Neighbors." In *Philosophical Dimensions of Parapsychology*, edited by Hoyt L. Edge and J. M. O. Wheatley, 374–87. Springfield, Ill.: Charles C. Thomas, 1976.

Bharati, A. *The Tantric Tradition.* London: Allen and Unwin, 1968.

Bhattacharya, Vidhushekara. *The Basic Conception of Buddhism.* Calcutta: University of Calcutta, 1934.

Binkley, R. "Philosophy and the Survival Hypothesis." *Journal of the American Society of Psychical Research* 60.1 (1966): 27–31.

Blacker, Carmen. "Other World Journeys in Japan." In *The Journey to the Other World*, edited by H. R. E. Davidson. Cambridge: D. S. Brewer, 1975.

Bloom, Alfred. *Shinran's Gospel of Pure Grace.* Tucson: University of Arizona Press, 1965.

Bok, Sisela. *Lying: Moral Choice in Public and Private Life.* New York: Pantheon Books, 1978.

[*The Tibetan*] *Book of the Dead.* Edited by W. Y. Evans-Wentz. Translated by Kazi Dawa-Samdup. London: Oxford University Press, 1957.

Broad, C. D. *Ethics and the History of Philosophy.* New York: Humanities Press, 1952.

Buchanan, Allen. "Medical Paternalism." *Philosophy and Public Affairs* 7 (Summer 1978): 370–90.

Buddhaghosa. *The Visuddhimagga of Buddhaghosacariya.* Cambridge: Harvard University Press, 1950.

Burnouf, Eugene. *Introduction à l'histoire du bouddhisme indien.* Paris: Maisonneuve et Cie, 1876.

Chai, Winberg. *The Story of Chinese Philosophy*. New York: Washington Square Press, 1961.

Chan, Wing-tsit. *An Outline and an Annotated Bibliography of Chinese Philosophy*. New Haven: Far Eastern Publications, Yale University, 1961.

Chan, Wing-tsit, and Burton Watson, eds. *Sources of Chinese Tradition*. New York: Columbia University Press, 1960.

Chang, Chen-chi. *The Practice of Zen*. New York: Harper, 1959.

Chappell, David. "Chinese Buddhist Interpretations of the Pure Lands." In *Buddhist and Taoist Studies*, 1. Edited by David Chappell and Michael Saso. Honolulu: University Press of Hawaii, 1977.

————. "The Formation of the Pure Land Movement in China: Tao-ch'o and Shan-tao." In *Berkeley Buddhist Studies*, 3. Edited by Michael Solomon. Forthcoming.

Ch'en, Kenneth K. S. *Buddhism in China*. Princeton: Princeton University Press, 1964.

Chih-pan. *A Chronicle of Buddhism in China, 581–960 A.D.* Translated and edited by Jan Yun Hua. Santiniketan: Visvabharati, 1966.

Chikamatsu, Monzaemon. *Major Plays of Chikamatsu*. Translated by Donald Keene. New York: Columbia University Press, 1961.

Childers, Robert Caesar, ed. *A Dictionary of the Pali Language*. 2 vols. London: Kegan Paul, Trench, Trubner and Co., 1875.

Coates, H. H., and Ryūgaku Ishizuka. *Hōnen the Buddhist Saint*. Kyoto: Chionin, 1925.

Colebrooke, Henry T. *Miscellaneous Essays*. 2 vols. Edited by E. B. Cowell. London: Trubner and Co., 1873.

Conze, Edward. *Buddhism: Its Essence and Development*. Oxford: Bruno Cassirer, 1951.

————. *Buddhist Wisdom Books*. London: Allen and Unwin, 1958.

Coomaraswamy, Ananda Kentish. *Buddha and the Gospel of Buddhism*. New York: Harper and Row, 1964.

Corless, Roger. "T'an-luan's Commentary on the Pure Land Discourse." Ph.D. diss., University of Wisconsin, 1973.

Bibliography

Creel, H. G. *Chinese Thought: From Confucius to Mao Tse-tung.* Chicago: University of Chicago Press, 1953.

Csoma de Koros, A. *Tibetan Studies.* Edited by E. Denison Ross. Calcutta: Baptist Mission Press, 1912.

Dahlke, Paul. *Buddhism and Its Place in the Mental Life of Mankind.* London: Macmillan, 1927.

Dainelli, Giotto. *Buddhists and Glaciers of Western Tibet.* New York: E. P. Dutton, 1934.

D'Alwis, James. *Buddhist Nirvāna: A Review of Max Müller's Dhammapāda.* Colombo, Sri Lanka: William Skeen, 1871.

David-Neel, Alexandra. "Le bouc émissaire des Thibétains." *Mercure de France* 124 (1917): 649–60.

———. *Buddhism: Its Doctrines and Its Methods.* London: John Lane, 1939.

———. *Mystiques et magiciens du Thibet.* Paris: Plon, 1930.

Davidson, H. R. E., ed. *The Journey to the Other World.* Cambridge: D. S. Brewer, 1975.

Day, Clarence Burton. *The Philosophers of China, Classical and Contemporary.* New York: Philosophical Library, 1962.

deBary, Theodore, ed. *The Buddhist Tradition.* New York: Modern Library, 1969.

deGroot, J. J. M. *The Religious System of China.* Taipei: Cheng Wen Publishers, 1972.

DeSilva, Lynn A. *The Problem of the Self in Buddhism and Christianity.* Colombo, Sri Lanka: Study Centre for Religion and Society, 1975.

deVisser, M. W. *Ancient Buddhism in Japan.* Leiden: E. J. Brill, 1935.

———. *The Bodhisattva Ti-tsang [Jizō] in China and Japan.* Berlin: Oesterheld and Co., 1914.

Digha Nikāya. In *Sacred Books of the Buddhists.* Translated by T. W. Rhys-Davids. London: Oxford University Press, 1899.

Ducasse, C. J. *A Critical Examination of the Belief in a Life after Death.* Springfield, Ill.: Charles C. Thomas, 1961.

Dumoulin, Heinrich. *History of Zen Buddhism.* Translated by Paul Peachey. New York: Pantheon Books, 1963.

Dutt, Nalinaksha. *Aspects of Mahāyāna Buddhism and Its Relation to Hīnayāna*. London: Luzac and Co., 1930.

———. *Early Monastic Buddhism*. Calcutta: Calcutta Oriental Book Agency, 1960.

Egbert, Lawrence, et al. "Reduction of Post-operative Pain by Encouragement and Instruction of Patients." *New England Journal of Medicine* 270.16 (1964): 825–27.

Ekvall, Robert K. *Religious Observances in Tibet*. Chicago: University of Chicago Press, 1964.

Ellam, J. E. *The Religion of Tibet*. New York: E. P. Dutton and Co., 1927.

Ellis, David. "The Chemistry of Psi." In *Parapsychology and the Sciences*. Edited by Alan Angoff and Betty Shapin, 209–24. New York: Parapsychology Foundation, 1974.

Evans-Wentz, W. Y. Introduction to *[The Tibetan] Book of the Dead*. Edited by W. Y. Evans-Wentz. Translated by Kazi Dawa-Samdup. London: Oxford University Press, 1957.

———. *Tibetan Yoga and Secret Doctrines*. London: Oxford University Press, 1935.

Foucaux, Philippe Edouard. *Doctrine des bouddhistes sur le nirvāna*. Paris: Benjamin Duprat, 1864.

Fujikoshi, Jikai. "Bannen no Hōnen Shōnin." *Indogaku Bukkyōgaku Kenkyū* 20.1 (Dec. 1971): 121–27.

Fujimoto, Ryūkyō. *An Outline of the Triple Sūtra of Shin Buddhism*. 2 vols. Kyoto: Hompa Honganji and Hyakkaen, 1955, 1960.

Fujino, Yoshio, ed. *Kanatehon Chūshingura: Kaishaku to Kenkyū*. Tokyo: Ofūsha, 1975.

Fujita, Kōtatsu. *Genshi Jōdō Shisō no Kenkyū*. Tokyo: Iwanami Shoten, 1970.

Fujiwara, Ryōsetsu. *Nembutsu Shisō no Kenkyū*. Kyoto: Nagata Bunshodo, 1957.

———. *The Way to Nirvana*. Tokyo: Kyōiku Shinchōsha, 1974.

Fung, Yu-lan. *A Short History of Chinese Philosophy*. New York: Macmillan, 1948.

——. *The Spirit of Chinese Philosophy*. Translated by E. R. Hughes. London: Kegan Paul, 1947.

Gert, Bernard, and Charles Culver. "Paternalistic Behavior." *Philosophy and Public Affairs* 6 (Summer 1976): 45–57.

Getty, A. *The Gods of Northern Buddhism*. Oxford: Clarendon Press, 1928.

Gordon, Antoinette K. *The Hundred Thousand Songs: Selections from Milarepa*. Rutland, Vt.: Charles E. Tuttle Co., 1961.

——. *The Iconography of Tibetan Lamaism*. New York: Columbia University Press, 1939.

Govinda, Anagarika. *Foundations of Tibetan Mysticism*. New York: E. P. Dutton, 1960.

Grimm, George. *The Doctrine of the Buddha*. 2d ed. Berlin: Akademie-Verlag, 1958.

Grosso, Michael. "Possible Nature of Post-Mortem States." *Journal of the American Society of Psychical Research* 74.4 (1980): 419–23.

——. "The Survival of Personality in a Mind-Dependent World." *Journal of the American Society of Psychical Research* 73.4 (1979): 367–80.

Guenther, H. V. *Life and Teaching of Naropa*. Oxford: Clarendon Press, 1963.

Hanayama, Shinshō. *History of Japanese Buddhism*. Translated by Kōsho Yamamoto. Tokyo: CIIB Press, 1960.

Harrer, H. *Seven Years in Tibet*. London: Rupert Hart-Davis, 1955.

Harrison, Jonathan. "Religion and Psychical Research." In *Philosophy and Psychical Research*. Edited by Shivesh C. Thakur, 97–120. London: George Allen and Unwin, 1976.

Hastings Encyclopedia of Religion and Ethics. Edited by James Hastings. New York: Charles Scribner's Sons, 1924.

Hermanns, Mathias. *Mythen und Mysterien, Magie und Religion der Tibeter*. Cologne: B. Pick, 1956.

Hick, John. *Death and Eternal Life*. New York: Harper and Row, 1976.

Hoffmann, Helmut. *The Religions of Tibet*. London: George Allen and Unwin, 1961.

Hoffmann, Helmut, et al. *Tibet: A Handbook.* Bloomington: Indiana University Research Center for the Language Sciences, 1975.

Hōnen Shōnin den Zenshū. Osaka: Hōnen Shōnin den Zenshū Kankōkai, 1967.

Hopkins, Jeffrey, and Lati Rinbochay. *Death, Intermediate State, and Rebirth in Tibetan Buddhism.* Ithaca, N.Y.: Snow Lion Publications, 1979.

Hori, Ichirō. *Kūya.* Tokyo: Yoshikawa Kobunkan, 1958.

Hoshino, Gembō. *Shinshū no Tetsugakuteki Rikai.* Kyoto: Hōzōkan, 1972.

Hua, Hsuan. *A General Explanation of "The Buddha Speaks of Amitabha Sutra."* San Francisco: Buddhist Text Translation Society, 1974.

Hui-hai. *The Path to Sudden Attainment.* Translated by John Blofeld. London: The Buddhist Society, 1948.

Iida, Tsunesuke. "Bioethicswa nanio nasunoka." In *Nihon Rinri Gakkai Kenkyū Happyō Yōshi* (Paper delivered at the Thirty-Ninth Annual Conference of the Japan Ethics Association, Waseda University, Tokyo, 14–15 Oct. 1988), 40–42.

Ikemoto, Jushin. *Daimuryōjukyō no Kyōrishiteki Kenkyū.* Kyoto: Nagata Bunshōdō, 1958.

Inge, W. R., et al., eds. *Radhakrishnan: Comparative Studies in Philosophy.* London: Allen and Unwin, 1951.

Inoue, Kaoru. *Gyōki.* Tokyo: Yoshikawa Kobunkan, 1958.

Ippen Goroku. Illustrations reproduced in Makio Takemura et al. *Ippen, Nihonteki naru mono wo megutte.* Tokyo: Shunjūsha, 1991.

Ishida, Mitsuyuki. *Nihon Jōdōkyo no Kenkyū.* Kyoto: Hyakkaen, 1952.

Ishii, Kyōdo. *Senchakushū no Kenkyū.* Kyoto: Heirakuji Shoten, 1951.

Jacobson, Nils O. *Life Without Death?* Translated by Sheila La Farge. New York: Delacorte Press, 1974.

Jacobson, Norman Pliny. *Buddhism, The Religion of Analysis.* New York: Humanities Press, 1965.

James, William. "Human Immortality." In *William James on Psychical*

Research. Edited by Gardner Murphy and Robert Ballou, 279–308. New York: Viking Press, 1960.

Jayatilleke, K. N. *The Message of the Buddha*. New York: The Free Press, 1974.

Jennings, J. G. *The Vedantic Buddhism of the Buddha*. Delhi: Motilal Banarsidas, 1947.

Jōdōshū Zenshū. Tokyo: Jōdōshū Shutten Kankōkai, 1910.

Kalupahana, David J. *Buddhist Philosophy: A Historical Analysis*. Honolulu: University Press of Hawaii, 1976.

———. *Causality: The Central Philosophy of Buddhism*. Honolulu: University Press of Hawaii, 1975.

———. *A History of Buddhist Philosophy*. Honolulu: University Press of Hawaii, 1991.

Kant, Immanuel. *Kritik d. Reinen Vernunft*. 2d ed. Leipzig: F. Meiner, 1906.

Kastenbaum, Robert. *Between Life and Death*. New York: Springer-Verlag, 1979.

Kawasaki, Shinjō. "Tōyō Kodai no Seimei Juyō." In *Nihon Rinri Gakkai Kenkyū Happyō Yōshi* (Paper delivered at the Thirty-Ninth Annual Conference of the Japan Ethics Association, Waseda University, Tokyo, 14–15 Oct. 1988), 26.

Keith, Arthur Berriedale. *Buddhist Philosophy in India and Ceylon*. Oxford: Clarendon Press, 1923.

Kern, Hendrik. *Histoire du bouddhisme dans l'Inde*. Translated by Gédéon Huet. 2 vols. Paris: E. Leroux, 1901, 1903.

Kiev, A. *Magic, Faith and Healing*. London: Collier-Macmillan, 1964.

Kikumura, Norihiko. *Shinran: His Life and Thought*. Translated by Ken'ichi Yokogawa. Los Angeles: Nembutsu Press, 1972.

Kimura, Kiyotaka. *Shoki Chūgoku Kegon Shisō no Kenkyū*. Tokyo: Shunjūsha, 1977.

Kimura, Rihito. "In Japan, Patients Participate but Doctors Decide." *Hastings Center Report* 16.4 (1986): 22–23.

King, F. *Sexuality, Magic and Perversion*. London: Spearman, 1971.

Kiyota, Minoru. "Buddhist Devotional Meditation: A Study of the Sukhāvatīvyūhapadesa." In *Mahāyāna Buddhist Meditation: The-*

ory and Practice, edited by Minoru Kiyota, 249–96. Honolulu: University Press of Hawaii, 1978.

Kurita, Isamu. *Ippen Shōnin, Tabi no Shisakusha*. Tokyo: Shinchōsha, 1977.

Lai, Whalen. "Tales of Rebirths and the Later Pure Land Tradition in China." In *Berkeley Buddhist Studies*, 3. Edited by Michael Solomon. Forthcoming.

Lalou, Marcelle. *Les religions du Tibet*. Paris: Presses Universitaires de France, 1957.

Larue, Gerald A. *Euthanasia and Religion: A Survey of the Attitudes of World Religions to the Right-to-Die*. Los Angeles: The Hemlock Society, 1985.

LaVallée Poussin, Louis de. *Bouddhisme: Opinions sur l'histoire de la dogmatique*. Paris: Gabriel Beauchesne et Cie, 1908.

———. *Le Dogme et la philosophie du bouddhisme*. Paris: Gabriel Beauchesne, 1930.

———. *Nirvāna*. Paris: Gabriel Beauchesne, 1925.

———. *The Way to Nirvana: Six Lectures on Ancient Buddhism as a Discipline of Salvation*. Cambridge: Cambridge University Press, 1917.

Law, Bimala Churn. *The Buddhist Conception of Spirits*. Varanasi: Bhartiya Publishers, 1974.

———. *Heaven and Hell in Buddhist Perspective*. Varanasi: Bhartiya Publishers, 1973.

Lee, Shao Chang. *Popular Buddhism in China*. Shanghai: Commercial Press, 1939.

LeShan, Lawrence. "Physicists and Mystics, Similarities in World-View." *Journal of Transpersonal Psychology* 1.2 (1969): 1–15.

Leuba, James Henry. *Psychology of Religious Mysticism*. London: Kegan Paul, 1929.

Lewis, H. D. *The Self and Immortality*. New York: Seabury Press, 1973.

Luk, Charles. "The Sutra of the Contemplation of Amitāyus." In *The Secrets of Chinese Meditation*, edited by Charles Luk. London: Rider and Company, 1964.

Bibliography

Magness, T. *Samma Samadhi*. Thonburi, Thailand: Bhasicharoen, 1955.

Mahāvagga. In *The Buddha and His Teachings*, edited and translated by Narada-Thera. Colombo, Sri Lanka: Vajiraramaya, 1964.

Majjhima Nikāya. Translated by Bhikkhu Silacara. Leipzig: Walter Markgraf, 1912; London: Arthur Probsthain, 1913.

Matsunaga, Daigan, trans. *The Foundation of Japanese Buddhism*. 2 vols. Tokyo: Buddhist Books International, 1976.

Matsuno, Junko. *Shinran*. Tokyo: Sanseidō, 1959.

Meditation on Amitāyus. Translated by Junjirō Takakusu. Oxford: Clarendon Press, 1894.

Milindapanha. Edited and translated by V. Trenckner. London: Luzac, 1962.

Miller, Robert J. *Monasteries and Culture Change in Inner Mongolia*. Wiesbaden: O. Harrassowitz, 1959.

Mills, D. E. *A Collection of Tales from Uji*. Cambridge: Cambridge University Press, 1970.

Mizuno, Seiichi, and Toshio Nagahiro, eds. *Yün-kang: The Buddhist Cave Temples of the Fifth Century* A.D. *in North China*. 16 vols. Kyoto: Jimbun Kagaku Kenkyūsho, 1952.

Mochizuki, Shinkō. *Bukkyō Kyōten Seiritsushi*. Kyoto: Hōzōkan, 1946.

———. *Shina Jōdo Kyōrishi*. Kyoto: Hōzōkan, 1942.

Moncrieff, Malcolm M. *The Clairvoyant Theory of Perception*. London: Faber and Faber, 1951.

Mori, Ōgai. *Takasebune*. Tokyo: Iwanami Bunko, 1978.

Morioka, Masahiro. "Nōshi towa nan deatta ka." In *Nihon Rinri Gakkai Kenkyū Happyō Yōshi* (Paper delivered at the Thirty-Ninth Annual Conference of the Japan Ethics Association, Waseda University, Tokyo, 14–15 Oct. 1988), 7.

Müller, Max, ed. *Sacred Books of the East*. Vol. 49. Oxford: Clarendon Press, 1894.

———. *Selected Essays on Language, Mythology, and Religion*. 2 vols. London: Longmans Green and Co., 1881.

Murphy, Gardner. "Field Theory and Survival." *Journal of the American Society of Psychical Research* 39.4 (1945): 181–209.

————. "Psychical Research and the Mind-Body Relationship," *Journal of the American Society of Psychical Research* 40.3 (1946): 189–207.

Murti, T. R. V. *The Central Philosophy of Buddhism.* London: George Allen and Unwin, 1955.

Myōe, "Zaijarin." In *Kamakura Kyū Bukkyō.* Vol. 15 of *Nihon Shisō Taikei.* Edited by Shigeo Kamata and Tanaka Hisao. Tokyo: Iwanami Shoten, 1971.

Nagao, Gadjin. "On the Theory of the Buddha Body." *Eastern Buddhist,* n.s. 4.1 (May 1973): 25–53.

Nakamura, Hajime. *A History of the Development of Japanese Thought,* 1. Tokyo: Kokusai Bunka Shinkōkai, 1967.

————. *Tōzai Bunka no Kōryū.* Tokyo: Shunjūsha, 1965.

Nakamura, Hajime, et al., ed. and trans. *Jōdō Sambukyō.* 2 vols. Tokyo: Iwanami Shoten, 1963, 1964.

Nakamura, Kyōko. *Miraculous Stories from the Japanese Buddhist Tradition.* Cambridge: Harvard University Press, 1973.

Narasu, P. Lakshmi. *The Essence of Buddhism.* Bombay: Thacker and Co., 1907.

Nebesky-Wojkowitz, R. *Oracles and Demons of Tibet.* The Hague: Mouton, 1956.

Needham, Joseph. *Science and Civilisation in China.* Vol. 2 of *History of Scientific Thought.* Cambridge: Cambridge University Press, 1956.

Nhat-Hanh, Thích. *The Lotus in the Sea of Fire.* London: S. C. M. Press, 1967.

Nihon Rinri Gakkai Kenkyū Happyō Yōshi. 39th Annual Conference, Waseda University, Tokyo, Japan, 14–15 Oct. 1988.

Nyanatiloka, Mahāthera. *Karma and Rebirth.* Colombo, Sri Lanka: Buddhist Publication Society, 1955.

Obry, Jean Baptiste François. *Du Nirvāna bouddhique en reponse à M. Barthelemy Saint-Hilaire.* Paris: Auguste Durand, 1863.

Ogasawara, Senshū. *Chūgoku Jōdōkyo no Kenkyū*. Kyoto: Heirakuji, 1951.

———. *Chūgoku Kinsei Jōdōkyōshi no Kenkyū*. Kyoto: Hyakka-en, 1963.

Ōhara, Nobuo. "Sei to Shi no Rinrigaku." In *Nihon Rinri Gakkai Kenkyū Happyō Yōshi* (Paper delivered at the Thirty-Ninth Annual Conference of the Japan Ethics Association, Waseda University, Tokyo, 14–15 Oct. 1988), 54–55.

Ōhara, Shōjitsu. "Chūgoku Senjutsu Setsu ni taisuru Ichi Gimon." In Ryūkoku Daigaku Series, 359, *Kammuryōjukyō to Jōdōron: Kangyō*. Kyoto: Ryūkoku Daigaku, 1958.

———. *Zendō Kyōgaku no Kenkyū*. Tokyo: Meiji Shoin, 1943.

Ōhashi, Shunnō. *Ippen*. Tokyo: Yoshikawa Kobunkan, 1983.

Oldenberg, Hermann. *Buddha, His Life, His Doctrine, His Order*. Translated by W. Hoey. London: Williams and Norgate, 1882.

Osis, Karlis, and Erlendur Haraldsson. *At the Hour of Death*. New York: Avon, 1977.

Pallis, Marco. *Peaks and Lamas*. New York: Alfred A. Knopf, 1940.

Pande, Govind Chandra. *Studies in the Origins of Buddhism*. Delhi: Motilal Banarsidas, 1957.

Parker, Adrian. *States of Mind*. New York: Taplinger, 1975.

Pas, Julian. "Dimensions in the Life and Thought of Shan-tao." Paper delivered at the Society for the Study of Chinese Religion, St. Louis, Mo., Oct. 1976.

———. "Shan-tao's Interpretations of the Meditative Vision of Amitāyus." *History of Religions* 14.2 (1974): 100–103.

Pole, Wellesley T. *Private Dowding*. London: J. M. Watkins, 1917.

Price, H. H. *Fifty Years of Psychical Research: A Critical Survey*. New York: Arno Press, 1975.

———. "Survival and the Idea of Another World." *Proceedings of the Society for Psychical Research* 50.182 (Jan. 1953): 1–25.

Prince, R., ed. *Trance and Possession States*. Montreal: Bucke Society, 1968.

Radhakrishnan, S. *Eastern Religions and Western Thought*. London: Oxford University Press, 1939.

Ramacharaka, Yogi. *The Life Beyond Death*. Chicago: Yogi Publication Society, 1940.

Rawlings, Maurice. *Beyond Death's Door*. Nashville: Thomas Nelson, 1978.

Reichelt, Karl L. *Truth and Tradition in Chinese Buddhism*. Translated by K. V. Bugge. Shanghai, 1928. Reprint. New York: Paragon Book Reprints, 1968.

Reischauer, August K. *Studies in Japanese Buddhism*. New York: Macmillan Co., 1917.

Reishauer, Edwin O., trans. *Ennin's Diary: The Record of a Pilgrimage to China in Search of the Law*. New York: Ronald Press Co., 1955.

Rhine, J. B. "Research on Spirit Survival Re-examined." *Journal of Parapsychology* 20.2 (June 1956): 121–31.

———. "The Science of Nonphysical Nature." In *Philosophy and Parapsychology*. Edited by Jan Ludwig, 117–27. Buffalo: Promethus, 1978.

Rhys-Davids, C. A. F. "A Historical Aspect of Nirvana." In *Wayfarer's Words*. 3 vols. London: Luzac and Co., 1940, 1941, 1942.

Rhys-Davids, T. W. *Buddhism: Its History and Literature*. New York: G. P. Putnam's Sons, 1926.

Rhys-Davids, T. W. and W. Stede, eds. *The Pali Text Society's Pali-English Dictionary*. London: Luzac and Co., 1921–1925.

Ring, Kenneth. *Life at Death*. New York: Coward, McCann and Geoghegan, 1980.

Rockhill, W. W. *Diary of a Journey Through Mongolia and Tibet, 1891 and 1892*. Washington, D.C.: Smithsonian Institution, 1894.

———. *Land of the Lamas*. New York: Century Co., 1891.

———. *The Life of the Buddha*. London: Paul, Trench, Trubner and Co., 1907.

Rowell, Teresina. "The Background and Early Use of the *Buddhaksetra* Concept." *Eastern Buddhist* 6 (1934): 199–246, 379–431; 7 (1937):131–69.

Ryūkoku Translation Center. *Jōdō Wasan*. Series 4. Kyoto: RTC, 1965.

———. *Kyō Gyō Shin Shō*. Series 5. Kyoto: RTC, 1966.

————. *Shoshin Ge.* Series 1. Kyoto: RTC, 1961.

————. *Tanni Sho.* Series 2. Kyoto: RTC, 1962.

Saint-Hilaire, Barthelemy. *The Buddha and His Religion.* 3d ed. Translated and edited by L. Ensor. London: George Routledge, 1895.

Samyutta Nikāya. Translated by C. A. F. Rhys-Davids. 5 vols. London: Pali Text Society, 1917–1930.

Sarathchandra, E. R. *The Buddhist Psychology of Perception.* Colombo, Sri Lanka: Ceylon University Press, 1958.

Schopen, Gregory. "Sukhāvatī as a Generalized Religious Goal in Sanskrit Mahāyāna Sutra Literature." *Indo-Iranian Journal* 19 (Aug.–Sept. 1977): 176–210.

Schrader, F. Otto. "On the Problem of Nirvana." *Journal of the Pali Text Society* (1904–5): 157–70.

Servadio, Emilio. "Mind-Body, Reality, and Psi." In *Brain/Mind and Parapsychology.* Edited by Betty Shapin and Lisette Coly, 233–41. New York: Parapsychology Foundation, 1979.

Seward, Jack. *Hara-Kiri: Japanese Ritual Suicide.* Tokyo: Charles E. Tuttle, 1968.

Shigematsu, Akehisa. "Ōjōden no Kenkyū." *Nagoya Daigaku Bungakubu Kenkyū Ronsho Shigakuhen* 8 (1960): 1–114.

Shinran. *Kyōgyōshinshō.* Translated by D. T. Suzuki. Kyoto: Shinshū Ōtaniha, 1973.

Silverman, A. J., et al. "Hallucinations in Neurologic Syndromes." In *Hallucinations,* edited by L. J. West. New York: Grune and Stratton, 1962.

Snellgrove, David. *Buddhist Himalaya.* Oxford: Bruno Cassirer, 1957.

Stcherbatsky, T. *Buddhist Logic.* 2 vols. Leningrad: Academy of Sciences of the USSR, 1932.

————. *The Central Conception of Buddhism and the Meaning of the Word "Dharma."* London: Royal Asiatic Society, 1923.

————. *The Conception of the Buddhist Nirvana.* Leningrad: Academy of Sciences of the USSR, 1927.

Stevenson, Ian. "Carington's Psychon Theory as Applied to Cases of the Reincarnation Type." *Journal of the American Society of Psychical Research* 67.2 (1973): 130–45.

————. *Children Who Remember Previous Lives.* Charlottesville: University Press of Virginia, 1987.

Story, Francis. *Rebirth as Doctrine and Experience.* Kandy: Buddhist Publication Society, 1975.

Suzuki, D. T. *A Miscellany on the Shin Teaching of Buddhism.* Kyoto: Shinshū Ōtaniha Shomusho, 1949.

————. *Outlines of Mahāyāna Buddhism.* New York: Schocken Books, 1963.

————. *Shin Buddhism.* New York: Harper and Row, 1970.

————. *Studies in the Lankāvatāra Sūtra.* London: Routledge and Kegan Paul, 1930.

————, trans. *The Kyōgyōshinshō.* Kyoto: Shinshū Ōtaniha, 1973.

Taishō Shinshū Daizōkyō. Edited by Junjirō Takayanagi et al. Tokyo: Taishō Shinshū Daizōkyō Kankōkai, 1962.

Takakusu, Junjirō. *Essentials of Buddhist Philosophy.* Honolulu: University Press of Hawaii, 1947.

Takemura, Makio, et al. *Ippen, Nihonteki naru mono wo megutte.* Tokyo: Shunjūsha, 1991.

Tamaki, Kōshiro. "Shi no Oboegaki." *Bukkyō Shisō* 10 (Sept. 1988): 465–75.

Tamura, Enchō. *Hōnen Shōnin den no Kenkyū.* Kyoto: Hōzōkan, 1972.

Tanabe, George. "Myōe Shōnin: Tradition and Reform in Early Kamakura Buddhism." Ph.D. diss., Columbia University, 1981.

T'an-luan. "A Short Essay on the Pure Land." Translated by Leo Pruden. *Eastern Buddhist,* n.s. 7.1 (May 1975): 74–95.

Tart, Charles C. "States of Consciousness and the State-Specific Sciences." *Science* 176 (12 June 1972): 1203–10.

Thomas, E. J. *The History of Buddhist Thought.* 2d ed. London: Routledge and Kegan Paul, 1948.

Tsujimoto, Tetsuo. *Genshi Bukkyō ni okeru Shōten Shisō no Kenkyū.* Kyoto: Kenshin Gakuen, 1936.

Tsukamoto, Zenryū. *Bukkyō no Shisō: Chūgoku Jōdo.* Vol. 8. Tokyo: Kadokawa Shoten, 1968.

———. *Tō Chūki no Jōdō Kyō.* Kyoto: Tōhō Bunka Gakuin Kyōto Kenkyūsho, 1933.

Tsukinowa, Kenryū. *Butten no Hihanteki Kenkyū.* Kyoto: Hyakka-en, 1971.

Tucci, Giuseppe. *Tibet, Land of Snows.* Translated by J. E. S. Driver. New York: Stein and Day, 1967.

———. *The Tombs of the Tibetan Kings.* Rome: Instituto Italiano per il Medio ed Estremo Oriente, 1950.

Tyrrell, G. N. M. *Apparitions.* London: Duckworth, 1953.

Udāna. Vol. 8 of *Minor Anthologies of the Pali Canon.* Translated by F. L. Woodward. London: Oxford University Press, 1948.

Ueda, Yoshifumi, ed. and trans. *Notes on the Essentials of Faith Alone* (Shinran's *Yuishinsho-mon'i*). Kyoto: Hongwanji International Center, 1979.

Uesugi, Bunshū. *Zendō Daishi oyobi Ōjō Raisan no Kenkyū.* Kyoto: Hōzōkan, 1931.

Upadhyaya, K. N. *Early Buddhism and the Bhagavad Gita.* Delhi: Motilal Banarsidas, 1971.

Vasubandhu. *Vimsakakārikā-prakarana.* Translated by Louis de La-Vallée Poussin. Louvain: Bureaux du Museon, 1912.

Vergara, Kyojo Ananda, trans. *Buddha Tells of the Infinite: AmidaKyō.* New York: American Buddhist Academy, 1973.

Waddell, Laurence Austine. *The Buddhism of Tibet, or Lamaism.* Cambridge: W. Heffer and Sons, 1934.

Waitzskin, Howard, and John Stoeckle. "The Communication of Information about Illness." *Advances in Psychosomatic Medicine* 8 (1972): 185–215.

Warren, Mary Anne. "Do Potential People Have Moral Rights?" *Canadian Journal of Philosophy* 7.2 (1978): 275–89.

Watsuji, Tetsuro, ed. *Hagakure.* Tokyo: Iwanami Bunko, 1970.

Wayman, Alex. "The Intermediate State Dispute." In *Buddhist Studies in Honor of I. B. Horner.* Edited by L. Cousins, A. Kunst, and K. R. Norman, 227–39. Dordrecht: D. Reidel, 1974.

West, L. J., ed. *Hallucinations.* New York: Grune and Stratton, 1962.

Wheatley, J. M. O. "Reincarnation, etc." In *Philosophical Dimensions of Parapsychology.* Edited by Hoyt L. Edge and J. M. O. Wheatley, 111–19. Springfield, Ill.: Charles C. Thomas, 1976.

Whorf, Benjamin Lee. *Language, Thought, and Reality.* Edited by John B. Carroll. Boston: MIT Press, 1959.

Woodroffe, John. "The Science of Death." Foreword to *[The Tibetan] Book of the Dead.* Edited by W. Y. Evans-Wentz. Translated by Kazi Dawa-Samdup. London: Oxford University Press, 1957.

Yamaguchi, Susumu. *Seshin no Jōdō Ron: Muryōjukyō Upadaisha Ganshoge no Shikai.* Kyoto: Hōzōkan, 1966.

Yamakami, Sōgen. *Systems of Buddhistic Thought.* Calcutta: University of Calcutta Press, 1912.

Yamamoto, Kōshō. *An Introduction to Shin Buddhism.* Ube: Karinbunko, 1963.

———. *Shinshū Seiten.* Honolulu: Hompa Hongwanji Mission of Hawaii, 1955.

Zaehner, R. C. *Mysticism, Sacred and Profane.* Oxford: Clarendon Press, 1957.

Zürcher, Erik. *The Buddhist Conquest of China.* Leiden: Brill, 1959.

Index

Index

Bardo, 92–93, 114; three stages of,
  96–100
Bardo service, 94
*Bardo Thodol. See Book of the
  Dead*
Bauddha, 35
Beloff, John, 115
Berkeley, Bishop, and idealism, 55,
  59, 115
Bettelheim, Bruno, 20
Bhagavad Gita, 38
Bhagavat, 70
Bhaisajya-guru, 89
Bioethics, in Japan, 126–31, 134–
  35
Bishamonten, 68
Blacker, Carmen, 75
Bodhi, 70
Bodhisattva, the, 38
Bodhisattvas: achieving nirvana,
  119, 121; and aiding suffering
  humans, 48; and Buddha fields,
  50; as having three bodies, 89;
  and Mahayana Buddhism, 3;
  and the Pure Land, 60, 67, 71;
  and the Recompense realm, 58;
  and the soul, 98; yogins becom-
  ing, after death, 101
Bok, Sisela, 145
Bon: as animism, 86; influence on
  Tibetan Buddhism, 86–88, 92–
  93; philosophy of, 85; shamans
  of, 86; and twin spirits, 85
Bon Buddhists, 88
Bon service, 94
Book of the Dead, 92–102, 117
Brahmajāta Sūtra, 4
Brahman, 4, 51
Brahmanism, 4, 25, 28, 33. *See
  also* Sāmkhya
Brain death, 128–29, 131, 133–34
Broad, C. D., 112–13, 118
Brush writing, 77
Buddha, the: and annihilation, 28–
  29, 35; and condemning medita-
  tive powers, 16; and creation,
  61; and death, 2, 135; deifica-
  tion of, 49; and direct vision, 7;
  and enlightenment, 69; and eter-
  nalism, 35; as influenced by

Hindu thought, 1–2, 33; and
  karma, 7–9, 38, 61, 139; and
  meditations, 1, 5, 7, 14, 48,
  135; and nirvana, 24, 26, 49,
  119, 136; and no-soul theory,
  5, 8, 11; and paranormal powers, 90; and rebirth, 7–8, 13–
  16, 23, 38, 124, 135; and retrocognition, 7; and self-centeredness, 7; silences of, concerning nirvana, 31, 35, 37, 42,
  119; and suffering, 1–2, 6–7,
  35, 38; and suicide, 136; and
  women, 43
Buddha fields (Buddhaksetra), 46,
  50–52, 101. *See also* Buddha
  lands; Buddha realms
Buddhaghosa, 11
Buddhahood, 97
Buddha lands, 51, 61. *See also* Buddha fields; Buddha realms
Buddha realms. *See also* Buddha
  fields; Buddha lands
Buddha: Sein Leben, seine Lehre
  (Oldenberg), 31
Buddhism: and the afterlife, 1, 46–
  62; and apparition bodies, 112;
  and asceticism, 51; and bioethics, 126–31, 134–35; and
  Brahmanism, 25; in China, 3,
  48, 51–52, 87, 127, 137; and
  Christianity, 25, 48, 81, 87,
  119, 121, 129; and conception,
  13–14; and cosmology, 50, 88–
  89, 104; and cultural modifica-
  tion, 3; and death, 1–3, 69, 94–
  95, 124, 127–29, 131–35, 146;
  and empiricism, 51, 63; and the
  ethics of death, 126–47; and euthanasia, 124, 127–28, 135–47;
  and Hindu thought, 47–48; and
  idealism, 82–83, 104, 114–17,
  121; and impermanence, 1, 6–
  7; and individual choice, 144–
  47; in Japan, 3, 87, 126–47;
  and meditations, 61, 63; nihilism of, 25, 42; and nirvana,
  119; and the view of the person, 16; philosophy of, 1–2, 7,
  39, 85; and reality, 16; and re-

Index

Godhika, 136
Govinda, Anagarika, 93
Greater Analysis of Deeds Sutra, 12
Greater Vehicle, the. *See* Mahayana Buddhism
Grimm, George, 11, 34
Grosso, Michael, 118–19
Guru, 94, 96. *See also* Bodhisatt-vas; Lama
Gyōki, 77

Harrison, Jonathan, 112
Heian period, 77, 138
Herukas, 99
Hick, John, 106–8, 118–19
Hiei, Mount, 65, 67–68
Hīnayāna school. *See* Theravādins
Hinduism: and apparition bodies, 112; and influence on the Bud-dha, 1–2, 33; and karma, 7, 69; and myths of heavens, 51; and the soul, 4, 9
Hōnen (Genku), 68–69, 71, 75, 77–78, 144
Hoppe, 34
Hot hells, 86
Hua, 55
Hua-yen Sūtra, 61
Hui-yuan, 66–67, 71, 73
Hui-yung, 73
"Human Immortality" (James), 111
Humans, as one of the six levels, 58

Idealist next world, 82–83, 104, 114–17, 121
Iida, Tsunesuke, 131–32
Impermanence, 1, 5–7
Indeterminism, 13
Indian Buddhism, 66, 81, 86
Indian philosophy, 3–4, 49, 106. *See also* Samkhya
Ippen, Saint, 138–39

Jacobson, Norman Pliny, 33–34
Jaina, 35
Jains, 69, 137
James, William, 111
Japanese Amidist, 68
Japanese Society for Dying with

Dignity (Songenshi, Kyōkai), 145–46
Japanese Tendai Buddhism, 65–66. *See also* Pure Land Buddhism: in Japan
Japan Ethics Association, 127–28
Jātaka, 136–37
Jayatilleke, 37, 42
Ji School, 139
Jizō, 75
Jōdō tradition, and death, 137, 148
Jungian archetypes, 103

Kalupahana, David, 37
Kamakura period, 138
Kamma, 7, 12, 16–17, 19
Kannon, 100–101
Kant, Immanuel, 111
Karma: and the Buddha, 7–9; and early Buddhism, 61; Hindu con-cept of, 7, 69; and the Jains, 69; and Mahayana Buddhism, 61; and the mind-only doctrine, 91; as part of rebirth, 7, 12, 20, 22, 36, 38; as part of reincarna-tion, 107; and spatiotemporal gaps, 15–18; winds of, 99
Karmic cravings, 97
Karmic energy, 13–14, 17
Karunā-pundarīka, 60
Kastenbaum, Robert, 162n.2
Kazuhiro, Anzai, 128–29
Kegon school, 69
Ketsujō Ōjōshū (Chingai), 68
Khandhās, 6, 9–11, 16, 19, 33–34, 40, 108, 145
Kieth, Arthur Berriedali, 34
Kimura, Kiyotaka, 160n.68
Kōben (Myōe), 68–69
Kōen, 68, 75
Konjaku Monogatari, 75
Kuddhakapatha, 48
Kūkhai, 144
Kumārajīva, 67
Kūya, 77, 138

Lai, Whalen, 74
Lama, 101–3. *See also* Bodhisatt-vas; Guru
Larger Pure Land Sutra, 52, 55,

Index

3, 48–49; and the Buddha, 24, 46, 49, 119; characteristics of, 49; as eternal life, 24, 28–34; as an ethical state, 24, 35–39; modern interpretations of, 24; and non-Buddhists, 103; as not annihilation, 30, 154n.36; as the Perfect Experience, 97; as a postmortem alternative, 23–46, 98, 101, 104, 121; in relation to the Pure Land, 54; and Vajrayāna Buddhism, 87–89; as the Vision of God, 119. *See also* Nirupadhisesa; Sopadhisesa
Nirvanic states, 119
Nirvanic transcendence, 102
Nissen, Nagamatsu, 144
Nonexistence, as escape from suffering, 24, 28, 35
No-soul, theory of, 5–8, 108. *See also* Anattā, theory of
Nyanatiloka, 13
Nying-ma-pa Buddhist school, 93
Nyūdō, Ajisaka, 138–40

Obry, Jean Baptiste François, 33
Ōhara, Nobuo, 132
Ōjō, 139
Ōjō Yōshū (Genshin), 68
Oldenberg, Hermann, 29, 31
Out-of-body-experiences (OBEs), 16, 67, 96, 105, 110, 112–14, 116, 121, 124, 127

Pali, 3, 24–25, 27, 34
Pali Canon, 37
Pali Text Society, 30
Panchen lama, 101
Pande, 10, 41–42
Parker's Law of reincarnation, 109
Petavatthu, 135
Piaget, 20
Positivism, 36, 82, 112, 117
Poussin, La Vallée, 29, 32, 42
Pretas, 48, 58
Price, H. H., 82–83, 102, 106, 118–19
Psyche, rebirth of, 2
Psychic body, 10
Psychic energy, 10

Puggalavādins, 10–11
Pure Consciousness, 97
Pure Land: access to, 52–54, 64, 76–77, 100, 102; as the afterlife, 45; description of, 52–56; discovery of, by oneself, 63–83; and doubters, 56; epistemology of, 46–47, 83; and the faithful, 56; and meditation, 59; objections to, 58; objective idealism of, 59–62, 104; ontology of, 46–47, 56–62, 72, 83; phenomenal forms in, 60; scriptural authority for, 52; as a state between samsara and nirvana, 54–55, 57, 59, 76; as the ultimate reality, 72; and wish fulfillment, 54–55
Pure Land Buddhism, 3; and the afterlife, 46–62; and Amida, 89, 94; in China, 47, 52, 65–67, 71–72, 76–77, 81; and Christianity, 81–82; and deathbed practices, 71–76; and idealist next world, 82–83, 114; and implications for modern scholarship, 79–83; in Japan, 47, 52, 65, 68–69, 71–72, 76–79; and justifying the Pure Land, 79; and medicine, 79–81; and salvation, 78; and secularization, 77. *See also* Mahayana Buddhism; Tibetan Buddhism; Vajrayāna Buddhism
Pure Land Sutras, 47, 70, 76. *See also* Larger Pure Land Sutra; Meditation on Amida Sutra; Smaller Pure Land Sutra

Radhakrishnan, 4, 11, 34
Ramacharka, 106
Ratnasambhava, 88, 97
Rebirth: Buddha's definition of, 7; determinants of, 12–15; in early Buddhism, 1–22, 51, 88; and identity, 8–15; importance of, 2–5; and overpopulation, 18–20; and philosophical difficulties with, 15–22; process of, 12–15, 109–10; and spatiotemporal

Index

Three Precious Ones, 56
Tibetan Buddhism, 3, 92; and Bon
  influences on, 86–88; and the
  Book of the Dead, 84–103; and
  death, 94–95, 129; and salva-
  tion, 3. *See also* Mahayana Bud-
  dhism; Tantric Buddhism; Vaj-
  rayāna Buddhism
Tibetan philosophy and religion be-
  fore Buddhism, 85–87
Tibetan worldview, 84–85, 92
Titans, as one of the six levels, 58
Tokugawa period, 141
Transcendental states, 117–19
Transempirical states, 37
Transformation realm, 58
Transmigrating souls, 11
Trikāya doctrine, 88–89
Triple World, 57–59, 61
Tsukamoto, 157n.12
Tucci, Giuseppe, 86, 98
Tusita heavens, 87, 100
Two Truths theory, 60
Tyrell, G. N. M., 115

Uji Shūi Monogatari, 75
Ullambana services, 87
Upadhyaya, K. N., 42–43
Upanisads, 10, 20, 19
U San Pe, 34

Vairocana, 88, 97
Vajiputtakas. *See* Puggalavādins
Vajrayāna Buddhism, 3, 87–91;
  and deathbed practices, 93–96;
  and the five Great Buddhas,
  88–89; and good and evil, 99;
  and mind-only doctrine, 90–91;
  philosophical issues of, 102–3;

and transcendence 100–102.
  See also Mahayana Buddhism;
  Tibetan Buddhism
Vajrayāna Lama, 91
Vasubandhu, 27, 52, 55, 59, 90
Vedanā, 6
Vedanta, 108
Vedantins, 36, 70, 107–8
Vedas, 4, 20, 47
Vimānavatthu, 135
Viññāna, 6, 10
Vipasyin, 25
Visual meditation, 88
Visudhimagga, 117, 131, 151n.1

Warren, Mary Anne, 132
Wheel of birth, 24. *See also* Cycles
  of rebirth; Samsara
White Lotus Society, 66–67, 71
Wisdom-holding deities, 98
World beyond form, 57–59
World Federation of the Right to
  Die Society, 134–35
World of desire, 57–59
World of form, 57–59
World of Highest Happiness, 64

Yamakami, 38
Yamarāja, 74–75, 86
Yoga, 90, 96
Yogācārabhumi, 11
Yogacara Buddhist school, 87, 90
Yoga meditation, 102
Yogic masters, 87
Yogic traditions, 61, 100
Yogin, 61, 92–93, 96–97, 101, 103

Zen Buddhism, 137, 141
Zoroastrianism, 81

CARL B. BECKER was born in Chicago and educated at the University of Chicago Laboratory School and Principia College. He received his M.A. in Asian philosophy and his Ph.D. in Asian and comparative philosophy from the East-West Center in Hawaii. He taught comparative philosophy at Southern Illinois University at Carbondale, at the University of Hawaii, and at National Osaka University and Tsukuba University in Japan. He is currently an associate professor of comparative cultures at Kyoto University in Japan. In 1983, Becker received the Robert Ashby Prize for his study of out-of-body experiences. In 1986, he received the SIETAR Award for Paramount Contribution to Intercultural Education, Training and Research, and in 1992, an Honorary Doctorate of Divinity from the London Institute for Applied Research.

His numerous books include *Christianity: History and Philosophy* (Tokyo: Eihōsha, 1984), *At the Border of Death: A Japanese Near-Death Experience* (Tokyo: Yomiuri Shinbunsha, 1992), and *Paranormal Experience and the Survival of Death* (Albany: SUNY Press, 1993). Becker is an editorial consultant, reviewer, and contributor to the *Journal of Near-Death Studies,* the *Journal of Mind-Body Science,* and other Japanese serial publications. His latest research concerns medical ethics, holistic and palliative medicine, and terminal care in Japan.